SIGNIFICANT
DECISIONS
OF THE
SUPREME COURT,
1977-1978 TERM

SIGNIFICANT DECISIONS OF THE SUPREME COURT, 1977-1978 TERM

Bruce E. Fein

American Enterprise Institute for Public Policy Research
Washington, D.C.

Bruce E. Fein is an attorney with the U.S. Department of Justice.

The views of the author do not necessarily represent those of the Department of Justice.

ISSN 0162–0444
ISBN 0–8447–3360–1

AEI Studies 257

Printed in the United States of America

CONTENTS

1

OVERVIEW

Offering some cheer to both proponents and opponents of affirmative action programs, the Supreme Court's pioneering exploration of its constitutional parameters in *Regents of the University of California* v. *Bakke*,[1] characterized the moderate course charted during its 1977–1978 term. Speaking with a muffled voice, the Court in *Bakke* invalidated a racial quota embraced by a state medical school to exclude white applicants from competing for sixteen places in the entering class. Five justices, however, endorsed the use of race as a positive factor in the design of admissions programs by institutions of higher education. Other important civil rights decisions revealed a comparable disharmony in jurisprudential themes.

In what would popularly be described as liberal rulings, the Court overruled one decision and cast aside the rationale of another as it enlarged the opportunities for recovery of damages against federal executive officials[2] and municipalities[3] for violations of constitutional rights. In addition, residential customers of municipal utilities were granted due process protection before any termination of service for nonpayment.[4] Female employees garnered protection against discrimination founded on childbearing under the Civil Rights Act of 1964[5] and won a reprieve from paying higher pension contributions than their male counterparts to offset their longer life expectancy.[6] The Court also removed a financial barrier to the vindication of con-

---

[1] 438 U.S. 265 (1978).
[2] Butz v. Economou, 438 U.S. 478 (1978).
[3] Monell v. Department of Social Services of the City of New York, 436 U.S. 658 (1978).
[4] Memphis Light, Gas and Water Division v. Craft, 436 U.S. 1 (1978).
[5] Nashville Gas Co. v. Satty, 434 U.S. 136 (1977).
[6] City of Los Angeles, Department of Water and Power v. Manhart, 435 U.S. 702 (1978).

1

stitutional rights in affirming an award of attorney's fees against a state under the Civil Rights Attorney's Fee Awards Act of 1976.[7]

On the other hand, the Court offered judicial officers and prosecutors an impenetrable shield against damages for constitutional infractions committed in the process of adjudication[8] and circumscribed the damages recoverable against executive and administrative officials who enjoy only a qualified immunity from suits founded on constitutional torts.[9] It embraced a crabbed construction of the due process clause in rejecting procedural due process challenges to the dismissal of a medical school student for academic reasons[10] and to the private sale of stored goods by a warehouseman to enforce a lien for nonpayment.[11] And the Court retreated from a series of equal protection rulings[12] that had shielded aliens from a host of discriminatory state statutes in sustaining a law that excluded aliens from a state's police force.[13]

The Court's First Amendment rulings carried important implications for the involvement of corporations in political campaigns, the delivery of legal services, and the ability of the press to uncover and to publicize the misdeeds of government. In striking down a Massachusetts statute that prohibited expenditures by corporations for the purpose of influencing a referendum on individual income taxes,[14] the Court placed under a constitutional cloud several state and federal statutes that forbid expenditures by corporations to influence elections for public office. In offering substantial First Amendment shelter to solicitation of clients by attorneys,[15] the Court may have unleashed forces that could revolutionize the delivery of legal services to the average consumer and drive down costs. And the Court's refusal to concede that the media constitutionally enjoy a greater right of access to government information[16] and greater shelter from government investigators[17] than is available to other persons

---

[7] Hutto v. Finney, 437 U.S. 678 (1978).

[8] Butz v. Economou, 438 U.S. 478 (1978); Stump v. Sparkman, 435 U.S. 349 (1978).

[9] Carey v. Piphus, 435 U.S. 247 (1978); Procunier v. Navarette, 434 U.S. 555 (1978); Robertson v. Wegmann, 436 U.S. 584 (1978).

[10] Board of Curators of the University of Missouri v. Horowitz, 435 U.S. 78 (1978).

[11] Flagg Bros., Inc. v. Brooks, 436 U.S. 149 (1978).

[12] See Nyquist v. Mauclet, 432 U.S. 1 (1977); In re Griffiths, 413 U.S. 717 (1973); Sugarman v. Dougall, 413 U.S. 634 (1973); Graham v. Richardson, 403 U.S. 365 (1971).

[13] Foley v. Connelie, 435 U.S. 291 (1978).

[14] First National Bank of Boston v. Bellotti, 435 U.S. 765 (1978).

[15] In re Primus, 436 U.S. 412 (1978); Ohralik v. Ohio State Bar Association, 436 U.S. 447 (1978).

[16] Houchins v. KQED, Inc., 438 U.S. 1 (1978); Nixon v. Warner Communications, Inc., 435 U.S. 589 (1978).

[17] Zurcher v. Stanford Daily, 436 U.S. 547 (1978).

could weaken the institutional role of the press as a bulwark against official misfeasance.

A procession of criminal law decisions during the 1977–1978 term echoed a familiar theme of the Burger Court: hostility toward the exclusion of reliable evidence at trial as a sanction for constitutional [18] or statutory violations. [19] The Court also bolstered investigatory and prosecutorial powers in holding that suspected traffic offenders may be routinely ordered out of their vehicles, [20] that telephone companies may be required to assist in the installation of a court-authorized pen register device, [21] and that prosecutors may reindict an accused on more serious charges if he declines to plead guilty to the offenses charged in the initial indictment. [22] These rulings were balanced by the Court's resistance to broadening the circumstances under which warrantless searches can survive Fourth Amendment scrutiny. [23] Finally, the Court struggled with an array of double jeopardy questions in an unsuccessful effort to expound the circumstances that permit government appeals or retrials in criminal cases. [24]

The Future of Affirmative Action

The decision in *Regents of the University of California* v. *Bakke* leaves largely unsettled the future of affirmative action programs that prefer blacks or other minorities in selecting applicants to higher educational institutions, in awarding government contracts, and in hiring in the private and public sectors. It may foreshadow wholesale constitutional endorsement of a sweeping array of preferential programs, including the use of racial quotas, so long as they are made conditional upon appropriate findings of societal discrimination. On the other hand, the decision could be confined to approving preferential treatment of minorities because of race only by institutions of higher education and only for the purpose of obtaining a diverse student

---

[18] See, for example, United States v. Ceccolini, 435 U.S. 268 (1978); Stone v. Powell, 428 U.S. 465 (1976); United States v. Janis, 428 U.S. 433 (1976); Harris v. New York, 401 U.S. 222 (1971).

[19] See, for example, Scott v. United States, 436 U.S. 128 (1978); United States v. Donovan, 429 U.S. 413 (1977); United States v. Giordano, 416 U.S. 505 (1974).

[20] Pennsylvania v. Mimms, 434 U.S. 106 (1977).

[21] United States v. New York Telephone Co., 434 U.S. 159 (1977).

[22] Bordenkircher v. Hayes, 434 U.S. 357 (1978).

[23] Michigan v. Tyler, 436 U.S. 499 (1978); Mincey v. Arizona, 437 U.S. 385 (1978); Marshall v. Barlow's Inc., 436 U.S. 307 (1978).

[24] Compare Arizona v. Washington, 434 U.S. 497 (1978); Swisher v. Brady, 438 U.S. 204 (1978); and United States v. Scott, 437 U.S. 82 (1978), with Burks v. United States, 437 U.S. 1 (1978); Sanabria v. United States, 437 U.S. 54 (1978); and Crist v. Bretz, 437 U.S. 28 (1978).

3

body. A frequently overlooked aspect of the *Bakke* decision was the view of five justices that Title VI of the Civil Rights Act of 1964 cannot tolerate affirmative action programs in federally funded educational institutions that would offend the equal protection clause of the Fourteenth Amendment. If the Court sharply curtails racial preferences under the equal protection clause, Title VI would offer no justification for any expansion. [25] Generally speaking, however, the *Bakke* decision revealed a preponderance of constitutionally favorable signs for proponents of affirmative action.

The *Bakke* case emerged from a challenge to a special admissions program operated by a state medical school. Sixteen places in an entering class of one hundred were set aside solely for applicants from minority groups, thereby sheltering them from competition offered by white applicants. Allan Bakke, a white applicant, was denied admission to the medical school solely because his race disqualified him from competing for one of the sixteen minority slots. He attacked the legality of the racial quota under Title VI of the Civil Rights Act of 1964 and the equal protection clause of the Fourteenth Amendment. Dividing into three voting blocs, the Supreme Court invalidated the quota of sixteen by a 5–4 vote, but endorsed the use of race as a positive factor by higher educational institutions in considering the applications of minority students.

Justice Powell, in an opinion speaking solely for himself, stood in the center of the other eight justices. Title VI, he observed, prohibits schools that receive federal funds (as the state medical school did) from practicing racial discrimination. Legislative history evinces a clear congressional intent, he added, to proscribe only those racial classifications that would offend the equal protection clause or the Fifth Amendment. Accordingly, Powell confronted the question of whether the racial quota of sixteen could survive equal protection scrutiny.

Racial and ethnic classifications, Powell declared, are inherently odious to a free people committed to equality before the law. This is true, he stated, even if such classifications are ostensibly for benign purposes. A so-called benign racial preference may advance the interests of a minority group at the expense of individuals within the group. Moreover, Powell noted, the preference may reinforce common stereotypes that disparage the ability of certain groups to achieve success in a competitive environment. Finally, he asserted, there is a measure of inequity in forcing innocent members of a majority

---

[25] The rationale of Katzenback v. Morgan, 384 U.S. 641 (1966) arguably could give constitutional blessing to congressionally mandated affirmative action programs that would run afoul of the equal protection clause in the absence of supporting legislation.

group to shoulder the burden of redressing the legacy of past discrimination inflicted on minorities. Accordingly, Powell concluded, the reservation of sixteen places for minorities could pass constitutional scrutiny only if furtherance of a compelling government interest required such action.

Under this standard, Powell rejected as insufficient three interests offered by the medical school to justify the contested racial quota. It is constitutionally illegitimate, he declared, to prefer members of any race solely to ensure a specified numerical representation within a student body. While acknowledging that racial quotas may be an appropriate remedy after "judicial, legislative, or administrative findings of constitutional or statutory violations," have been made, Powell noted that the medical school had not predicated its special admissions program on such findings. The racial quota, therefore, could not be justified as a remedy to overcome the effects of past racial discrimination. The claim that the quota was necessary in order to improve the delivery of medical services to underserved communities was deficient, Powell declared, because more precise and reliable methods exist for selecting the applicants most likely to advance this goal.

Powell agreed, however, that institutions of higher education have a compelling interest in seeking a diverse student body. In pursuing this goal, he stated, race may be considered as a "plus" factor in an applicant's file. But race may not be used, Powell stressed, to insulate a minority applicant from competition offered by others who possess qualities that would similarly enhance student diversity and educational pluralism. Such qualities would include exceptional personal talents, unique work or service experience, leadership potential, maturity, demonstrated compassion, a history of overcoming disadvantage, or ability to communicate with the poor. Since setting aside sixteen minority slots excluded consideration of white applicants who could make an equal contribution to genuine student diversity, Powell concluded that the quota was unconstitutional.

Justice Brennan, joined by White, Marshall, and Blackmun, voted to exonerate the racial quota of any legal taint. Brennan concurred in Powell's conclusion that Title VI of the Civil Rights Act of 1964 proscribes racial discrimination that would also be constitutionally infirm under the equal protection clause. Unlike Powell, however, Brennan declared that "benign" racial classifications intended to further remedial purposes can survive equal protection scrutiny if these classifications are "substantially related" to the achievement of "important governmental objectives."

In order to remedy the effects of the past societal discrimination,

Brennan stated, the medical school was justified in preferring minority applicants over white applicants. This conclusion was supportable, Brennan asserted, because there exists a sound factual basis for concluding that underrepresentation of minorities in the medical profession is substantial and chronic and that the legacy of past discrimination handicapped minorities in competing for places in medical schools. The use of a racial quota was to some extent related to overcoming the effects of past discrimination, Brennan explained, because proxies of disadvantage other than race, such as poverty or family educational background, would for the most part assist white persons and because only minorities likely to have been isolated from the mainstream of American life were beneficiaries of the quota. Accordingly, he declared, the equal protection clause did not invalidate the medical school's reservation of sixteen positions solely for minorities.

Justice Stevens, joined by Justices Burger, Stewart, and Rehnquist, declined to address the constitutionality of the contested admissions program. Stevens concluded that the program ran afoul of Title VI of the Civil Rights Act of 1964 by discriminating against white applicants on the basis of race. He voiced no opinion as to whether the proscription of Title VI against racial discrimination was congruent with constitutional principles of nondiscrimination.

The combination of Powell's vote resting on the equal protection clause and the votes of Stevens, Burger, Stewart, and Rehnquist resting on Title VI invalidated the medical school's racial quota and resulted in Bakke's admission. The views expressed by Powell, Brennan, White, Marshall, and Blackmun, however, approved the use of a less rigid minority preference in admissions programs adopted by institutions of higher education. A narrow reading of Powell's opinion suggests that such preferences are valid only if embraced in a genuine quest for a diverse student body. This rationale, however, endorses racial preferences for an unlimited time, even after the lingering effects of past societal discrimination have dissipated.

There is a substantial basis, moreover, for concluding that the voting alignment in *Bakke* and the affirmative action principles espoused in the opinions of Brennan and Powell foreshadow broad constitutional endorsement of racial preference, including quotas, in areas where minorities are chronically and substantially underrepresented. The opinion of Justice Brennan indicated that minority preferences can be justified in any area of public life where it can reasonably be surmised that past societal discrimination has placed minorities at a competitive disadvantage. It is reasonable to assume, the opinion suggested, that slavery and historic discrimination

6

against minorities in public and private education and employment have lingering effects on the present generation of minorities that can justify discrimination in their favor. [26] If this view were to be adopted by one of the four justices—Stevens, Stewart, Burger, and Rehnquist—who declined to address the constitutionality of affirmative action in *Bakke*, then a majority of the Court would probably absolve from constitutional reproach virtually all the myriad programs of the federal government in which special preferences are granted to minorities in order to rectify past discrimination. If none of these justices joins the Brennan bloc of four, sweeping affirmative action programs may nevertheless receive the Court's cachet, with the vote of Justice Powell, if appropriate judicial, legislative, or administrative findings of historic discrimination against minorities in education and employment are made. There seems abundant evidence for making such findings. [27]

Of course, the fact that affirmative action programs can pass constitutional muster does not mean that they can marshal the political and public support necessary for their adoption. None of the justices in *Bakke* suggested that the Constitution requires affirmative action programs to compensate for historical racial discrimination. Public opinion polls have revealed a lack of support among voters for affirmative action programs that involve racial quotas and foretell difficulties in the creation or expansion of affirmative action programs.

Solicitation by Attorneys and the Delivery of Legal Services

In *Bates* v. *State Bar of Arizona*, 433 U.S. 350 (1977), the Court held that protection of commercial speech under the First Amendment could not countenance a state prohibition against the truthful newspaper advertising of routine legal services. That decision spurred greater price competition and the expansion of legal clinics that cater to clients with such ordinary problems as drafting a will or procuring a divorce. The constitutional shelter offered to the solicitation of clients by attorneys in *In re Primus*, 436 U.S. 412 (1978), and *Ohralik* v. *Ohio State Bar Association*, 436 U.S. 447 (1978), coupled with the proliferation of new attorneys, may accelerate the transformation in

---

[26] In a recent study the conclusion was offered that simple antibias policies will not lead to economic parity between whites and blacks in the foreseeable future because the latter are handicapped by a disadvantageous family structure, low social origins, and the burden of past discrimination. See Richard Freeman, "Black Economic Progress since 1964," *The Public Interest*, no. 52 (Summer 1978).

[27] See, for example, Oregon v. Mitchell, 400 U.S. 112 (1970); South Carolina v. Katzenback, 383 U.S. 301 (1966).

the delivery of legal services to consumers that *Bates* has spawned. In a decade, it may be commonplace to find attorneys soliciting individual clients and offering laymen advice as to their legal rights in a variety of settings. [28]

In *Primus,* a member of the South Carolina Bar was publicly reprimanded for disclosing in a letter to a woman who had been sterilized, Williams, that free legal services would be offered by the American Civil Liberties Union (ACLU) if she chose to seek damages against her physician. The disciplined attorney and her associates were affiliated with the ACLU, a nonprofit organization, but she received no compensation for work on its behalf. The letter was written after the attorney had addressed a group of mothers who were alleged to have been sterilized as a condition of continued receipt of Medicaid, advised them of their legal rights, and suggested the possibility of a lawsuit. Upon receiving a negative response from Williams, the attorney ceased any further solicitation. In soliciting a client for the ACLU when her associate served as staff counsel to the organization, the state supreme court ruled, the attorney had violated a disciplinary rule of the South Carolina Canons of Professional Ethics.

Voting 7–1 for reversal, the U.S. Supreme Court held that the questioned solicitation was shielded from disciplinary rebuke under the First Amendment. Writing for the Court, Justice Powell explained that *NAACP* v. *Button,* 371 U.S. 415 (1963), and its progeny had established the principle that collective activity in seeking effective access to the courts may be constitutionally curtailed only by narrowly tailored rules necessary to vindicate a strong government interest. He noted that in *Button,* the Court found constitutionally impeccable the activities of members and staff lawyers of the NAACP in advising blacks of their legal rights, urging them to file suits of a particular kind, recommending particular lawyers, and financing the ensuing litigation. The solicitation of black clients, the *Button* Court stressed, was for the purpose of furthering the civil rights objectives of the

---

[28] There is abundant evidence that unjustified fear of high cost is a substantial deterrent to the utilization of legal services by low- and middle-class consumers. The Report of the Special Committee on the Availability of Legal Services, adopted by the House of Delegates of the American Bar Association, concluded that "the actual or feared price of such services coupled with a sense of unequal bargaining status is a significant barrier to wider utilization of legal services." In another recent study it was shown that middle-class consumers overestimate lawyers' fees by 91 percent for the drawing of a simple will, 340 percent for reading and advising on a two-page installment sales contract, and 123 percent for thirty minutes of consultation. A substantial percentage of consumers are also discouraged from seeking legal advice by the inability to discern which lawyers are competent to handle their particular problems. See generally Bates v. State Bar of Arizona, 433 U.S. 350 at 370–71 (1977), nn. 22 and 23.

NAACP and its members and was tantamount to the exercise of expressive and associational freedoms at the core of the First Amendment's protective ambit. Justice Powell concluded that fidelity to the *Button* rationale required the grant of constitutional protection to the disciplined attorney's solicitation of a client for the ACLU for which she received no compensation.

The ACLU, Powell declared, engaged in litigation as a form of political expression, complemented by extensive educational and lobbying activities, in order to advance its well-established objectives with respect to civil liberties. The contested solicitation, he noted, was a vehicle for expressing the political beliefs of the attorney and for advancing the goals of the ACLU. First Amendment protection for the solicitation was not forfeited, Powell asserted, simply because the ACLU might have been awarded attorney's fees if a lawsuit commenced under its sponsorship was successful. Since litigation is an important avenue for advancing the pursuit of civil liberties and its effectiveness often turns on locating willing and suitable litigants, Powell explained, the solicitation was a form of associational and expressive freedom that could be restrained only by disciplinary rules narrowly intended to advance a compelling state interest.

The South Carolina rules invoked to condemn the solicitation, Powell stated, were overbroad and, as applied, failed to advance the state's legitimate interests in preventing undue influence, overreaching, misrepresentation, invasion of privacy, conflict of interest, lay interference with the attorney-client relationship, and undue commercialization. Powell observed that the questioned letter conveyed information, offered no real opportunity for overreaching, and involved little invasion of privacy. In addition, he noted, the record failed to disclose any serious conflict of interest or lay interference by the ACLU in the litigation it sponsored. And there is no threat of undue commercialization of legal practice, Powell asserted, when free legal services to indigents are offered by a nonprofit organization. Accordingly, the Court overturned the disciplinary sanction, rejecting the proposition that sweeping prophylactic rules may be applied to forestall solicitation of clients that is part and parcel of political expression and association.

In *Ohralik*, a unanimous Court (Justice Brennan not participating) held that an attorney may be disciplined for soliciting clients in person, for pecuniary gain, under circumstances that imperil substantial state interests. The facts of the case, however, suggest important limitations on the holding.

An attorney made an unsolicited visit to the parents of an eighteen-year-old victim of an automobile accident and learned that their

9

daughter had been hospitalized. He then approached the daughter while she was lying in traction in her hospital room and quickly sought a representation agreement. Demurring, she expressed a desire to consult her parents.

Concealing a tape recorder, the attorney then revisited the parents and explained the insurance rights of their injured daughter and her companion who had also been hurt in the accident. Two days later, the attorney returned to the hospital and obtained the daughter's signature on a contract entitling him to a third of any recovery. He next obtained the name and address of the injured companion, also aged eighteen, made an unsolicited visit to her home with a concealed tape recorder, explained her insurance rights, and received her consent to his offer to represent her for a contingent fee of a third of any recovery.

Thereafter, both the representation agreements were repudiated and complaints against the attorney were filed with a grievance committee of a county bar association. At the final stage of the disciplinary process, the attorney was suspended indefinitely by the Ohio Supreme Court for violating antisolicitation rules. Affirming the suspension, the U.S. Supreme Court rejected the contention that the disciplinary sanction offended the First Amendment guarantee of freedom of speech.

The Court stated that personal solicitation of clients for commercial gain is entitled to some First Amendment protection. It noted, however, that the hazards created by solicitation in person far exceed those posed by the newspaper advertising of routine legal services endorsed in *Bates*. The former may exert pressure on the prospective client to reach a quick decision without opportunity for comparison, reflection, or information from disinterested sources. Solicitation in person, the Court thus concluded, deserves lesser constitutional protection than the advertising protected in *Bates* because it may inhibit informed and reliable decisionmaking by clients.

The Court also observed that the Ohio ban on personal solicitation of clients served to forestall fraud by attorneys, undue influence, intimidation, overreaching, and other vexatious conduct. It reasoned that solicitation in person for pecuniary gain was sufficiently likely to beget these evils to justify a prophylactic prohibition without requiring specific proof of actual overreaching or other misconduct as a foundation for imposing sanctions on a wayward attorney. Proof of actual harm would be difficult, the Court declared, because solicitation in person is not ordinarily open to public scrutiny and evidence of what transpired between the attorney and client would frequently consist of unreliable memories. Accordingly, the Court concluded that the attorney could be constitutionally disciplined for commercial solicitation in person that merely threatened a legitimate state interest.

The contested solicitation clearly created such a threat. The attorney approached two young victims of an accident when they were especially susceptible to influence. Services were offered under contingency-fee arrangements that sounded free of cost to the uninformed youths, and a concealed tape recorder was used under circumstances conducive to overreaching. Since the solicitation in person endangered state concerns about fraud, undue influence, and other vexatious conduct, the Court held that it was not protected by the First Amendment against state sanction.

The *Primus* and *Ohralik* decisions may spur widespread use of solicitation of clients in person for two reasons. First, the unmistakable teaching of *Primus* is that nonprofit public-interest organizations that litigate in pursuit of political or ideological goals enjoy broader First Amendment protection in soliciting clients than can be claimed by the overwhelming majority of attorneys who are profit-oriented. A number of these attorneys, especially those practicing as individuals or in small groups, are thus constitutionally handicapped in competing for clients who may also be solicited by public-interest attorneys. They may, therefore, seek to eliminate broad state prohibitions on solicitation in person to remove this competitive disadvantage.

Second, *Ohralik* suggests that solicitation of clients in person by profit-seeking attorneys is constitutionally protected so long as no potential for overreaching, wrongdoing, or invasion of privacy is threatened. *Ohralik* provides a firm basis for arguing, for example, that an attorney could not be disciplined for soliciting clients among landlords or tenants in a city subject to rent controls in the following manner:

1. Television, radio, and newspaper advertisements invite the prospective clients to a group meeting where their legal rights under a rent-control ordinance and possible litigation will be discussed. (The advertising minimizes any invasion of privacy and group solicitation diminishes the likelihood of undue influence.)

2. A verbatim record is maintained of all that transpires at the meeting and a copy is maintained for inspection by any grievance or disciplinary committee. All in attendance are informed of these facts. (The verbatim record will facilitate resolution of any charges of actual misconduct.)

3. All representation agreements that emerge from the meeting offer the client a seven-day cooling-off period during which the agree-

ment may be revoked. (The cooling-off period offers the client an opportunity to shop for other attorneys and to reflect on the wisdom and necessity for legal representation. It thus dispels any charge that the representation agreement was obtained in a fashion that disserved First Amendment values.)

The current flood of attorneys into the legal market may cause the embrace of solicitation schemes similar to that described above in a search to expand the demand for legal services.

Corporate Free Speech and Political Expenditures

The growth of government regulation has tied the financial health of an increasing number of corporations to the political process. Their ability to influence the legislative and executive branches, however, is at present circumscribed by several laws that prohibit expenditures by corporations in connection with elections for public office. [29] The decision in *First National Bank of Boston* v. *Bellotti*, 435 U.S. 765 (1978), however, may have sounded the death knell of these prohibitions. There the Court overturned a state criminal statute that banned corporate expenditures intended to influence referendum proposals that do not materially affect corporate interests. The statute presumed conclusively that individual income tax referenda could not have a material effect on any corporation. It was assailed by corporations that united to publicize their views on a proposal subject to a referendum that would have authorized the imposition of a graduated individual income tax.

Justice Powell, speaking for a 5–4 majority, declared that speech sponsored by corporate funds is sheltered by the First Amendment if it advances public debate of government affairs. Debate over the desirability of individual income tax proposals, he noted, falls squarely within this protection. A state may curtail such speech, Powell said, only when it is necessary in order to vindicate a compelling countervailing interest. The two justifying interests proffered by the state, he explained, failed to satisfy this exacting standard.

The first was a desire to encourage individual participation and confidence in the political process. Attainment of these goals might be frustrated, it was urged, if corporations exercised undue influence in the discussion of an issue subject to a referendum through the expenditure of corporate funds. Powell explained, however, that the First Amendment cannot tolerate suppression of speech either because the speech may be convincing or because the suppression is

---

[29] See, for example, 2 U.S. Code 441b.

necessary to enhance the voice of other participants in the political process. Moreover, he emphasized, there was no showing that corporate influence had been significant in referenda or had threatened the confidence of the citizenry in government.

The second interest advanced to justify suppression of corporate speech was the protection of shareholders against political expenditures they might oppose. Powell noted, however, that corporate expenditures in referenda were prohibited irrespective of the wishes of shareholders. Moreover, he observed, corporate expenditures to lobby for the passage or defeat of legislation were permitted without regard to the views of shareholders. Accordingly, Powell concluded, the interest of the state in protecting shareholders was too much attenuated to justify its selective prohibition on the use of corporate funds to influence the outcome of an income tax referendum.

A central teaching of *First National Bank* is that corporate expenditures that contribute to political discussion or the marketplace of political ideas are entitled to powerful First Amendment protection. Corporate expenditures intended to influence elections for public office would seem to be entitled to comparable protection. [30] Wholesale bans on corporate expenditures in such elections can survive attack under the First Amendment, Powell suggested, [31] only if they are founded on legislative findings that they would corrupt or create the appearance of corrupting the political process. Making these findings seems problematic because reasonable ceilings on corporate expenditures appear to be sufficient to forestall political corruption or its appearance.

Warrants to Search Newsrooms

A recurrent theme in the 1977–1978 term was that neither the press nor broadcasters are constitutionally endowed with special privileges either to gather or withhold information of public or government interest. This theme appeared in *Zurcher* v. *Stanford Daily*, 436 U.S. 547 (1978), in which it was held that neither the press nor other innocent persons have a constitutional right to compel investigators to demonstrate the futility of a subpoena before resorting to a warrant to search their premises for evidence of crime. There has been widespread condemnation of the *Zurcher* ruling by representatives of the media, legislators, and others. Even the local judge who signed the contested search warrant in *Zurcher* characterized the decision as a

---

[30] See Buckley v. Valeo, 424 U.S. 1 (1976), 19–20, 44–49.
[31] 435 U.S. at 788, n. 26.

threat to the First Amendment and has called for remedial legislation. The criticism heaped upon *Zurcher* seems overstated, however, and a cautious approach toward legislative curtailments of search warrants seems justified.

The *Zurcher* case stemmed from a violent confrontation between police and demonstrators in the Stanford University Hospital in which nine officers were assaulted. Photographs in an ensuing edition of the *Stanford Daily*, a student newspaper, gave the police probable cause to believe that the *Daily* possessed negatives, film, and pictures that would identify the assailants of the police. A warrant was issued by a magistrate authorizing the police to search the *Daily's* offices for such materials, despite the absence of allegations that the *Daily* or its staff were involved in wrongdoing.

The search occurred in the presence of *Daily* staff members and covered photographic laboratories, filing cabinets, desks, and wastepaper baskets. It offered police officers an opportunity to read some of the *Daily's* notes and correspondence. Whether they had taken advantage of the opportunity was disputed, and the police were not advised by the staff that confidential materials were contained in the areas they were searching.

Although no probative evidence was uncovered in the search, the constitutionality of the warrant was challenged in federal district court. It held that the Fourth Amendment, as applied to the states through the Fourteenth Amendment, forbids the use of warrants to search the premises of innocent persons for evidence of crime unless there is probable cause to believe that a *subpoena duces tecum* would be impracticable. In addition, the district court held that when an innocent newspaper is the object of the search, a warrant could be constitutionally tolerated only upon a clear showing that important materials would be destroyed or removed from the jurisdiction and that a restraining order would be ineffective. Since these conditions were not satisfied before issuance of the questioned warrant, the search of the *Daily's* offices was declared unconstitutional. The court of appeals affirmed, but the Supreme Court reversed by a vote of 5–3.

Writing for the majority, Justice White explained that neither the language of the Fourth Amendment nor precedent justified circumscribing the use of warrants to search the premises of nonsuspects for evidence of crime. Valid warrants to search the property of any person, he stated, may be issued when a magistrate finds probable cause to believe that fruits, instrumentalities, or evidence of crime is located there. Insisting that a *subpoena duces tecum* be employed to obtain evidence from nonsuspects, White asserted, could frustrate many criminal investigations. The seemingly innocent person might not turn out to be innocent at all, or might be so sympathetic to the culpable persons that he would assist in the destruction or removal of the criminal evidence after receipt of a subpoena. In addition, the evidence could disappear during litigation in which the validity of the subpoena was challenged. On the other hand, White asserted, the availability of warrants to search the premises of nonsuspects does not endanger privacy values because subpoenas are ordinarily used when cooperation is anticipated. Subpoenas, he noted, are generally preferred over warrants by investigators because they do not involve the judiciary or proof of probable cause.

The First Amendment, White stated, does not endow the press with any greater shield against search warrants than is enjoyed by individuals. White acknowledged that a warrant must describe the items to be seized and the places to be searched with "particular exactitude" when the warrant's execution could threaten First Amendment concerns. However, he stated, there is no constitutional justification for invalidating warrants to search the premises of a newspaper simply because they might cause self-censorship or dry up some confidential sources of information. Accordingly, White concluded, the search of the *Daily*'s offices was unobjectionable under both the Fourth and First amendments.

Critics of the *Zurcher* ruling have argued that it licenses the police to rummage at large through newspaper files and to harass disfavored members of the media. Candor in editorial deliberations and investigative reporting, it is said, are imperiled by the decision. These fears, however, are open to question. Justice White expressly denied that the decision empowered "officers to rummage at large in newspaper files or to intrude into or to deter normal editorial and publication decisions." Moreover, he suggested, if experience discloses the abuse of search warrants against the media, additional constitutional protections might be erected. White also noted that the needless use of a search warrant to harass the press or for other improper purposes might render it constitutionally vulnerable even if use of the warrant was founded on probable cause. Unless White was disingenuous in making these assertions, it seems premature to interpret *Zurcher* as a constitutional license for police to rummage through newsrooms.

Some have said that *Zurcher* endorsed the method used by the police to execute the contested warrant, which involved a sweeping search of the *Daily*'s offices and an opportunity to examine confidential papers outside the scope of the warrant. Thus, it is argued, comparable exposure of confidential information during the execution of search warrants is threatened in all news offices. But it seems doubtful that the Court in *Zurcher* voiced any opinion on the legality of the execution of the search warrant. Neither the district court nor the court of appeals rested its condemnation of the search on deficiencies in executing the warrant. The Supreme Court, moreover, found it unnecessary to determine whether police officers had in fact read confidential and irrelevant notes and correspondence during the search of the *Daily*'s premises. It seems unlikely that the Court would have decided the legality of the execution of the search warrant without resolving this dispute. Finally, Justice Powell in his concurring opinion warned that "there is no reason why police officers executing a warrant should not seek the cooperation of the subject party, in order to prevent needless disruption." Since the police did not seek the cooperation of the *Daily*'s staff members in executing the warrant, it is unlikely that Powell would have joined the majority opinion if he had thought it had constitutionally vindicated the manner of executing the warrant. In sum, there seems substantial room for argument that *Zurcher* left open the question of whether police may execute warrants in a manner that threatens to expose confidential information outside the scope of the warrant.

Whether justified or not, fears that the *Zurcher* decision endangers individual privacy and a free press has prompted calls for remedial legislation and the enactment of a California statute[32] to restrict the use of search warrants. Several bills were introduced in the 95th Congress[33] that would prohibit the issuance of a warrant to search the premises of the print or broadcast media for evidence of crime absent a showing that a subpoena would beget the destruction or removal of the evidence. It is said that this rule harmonizes fairly the competing public interests in effective enforcement of criminal law and a vigorous press undaunted in its scrutiny of government. But there may be problems in implementing the rule. If search warrants are in fact to be available in circumstances in which a subpoena would frustrate a criminal investigation, then the police would seem to be justified in maintaining files on members of the media to permit a reasoned evaluation of their hostility or sympathy toward enforcement of particular criminal statutes or criminal laws generally. The police may be especially inclined to compile such dossiers on members of the so-called antiestablishment media or pamphleteers who voice support for revolutionary or terrorist groups or activities. The compilation and maintenance of such files, however, might chill the exercise of First Amendment rights. But if such files were prohibited,

---

[32] See West's California Penal Code, section 1524(c).

[33] See *News Media and The Law*, vol. 2, no. 3 (October 1978), p. 20, published by the Reporters Committee for Freedom of the Press.

the police would be cut off from the information necessary to demonstrate that a subpoena in lieu of a search warrant would probably abort a criminal investigation. The prohibition would thus undercut the public interest in effective enforcement of the criminal law.

When faced with a choice between possible abuses stemming from police dossiers and those associated with search warrants, the media and the Congress might rationally perceive the latter as the greater problem. Nevertheless, recent history teaches that the former threat should not be discounted as illusory when a statute to serve the public interest is being drafted.

Voting Alignments

Members of the present Court have established voting patterns that are on the whole predictable in cases concerning the administration of criminal justice and a broad spectrum of issues having to do with civil rights and civil liberties. Generally speaking, the votes of Rehnquist and Burger are cast in favor of the government and against claims of civil rights or civil liberties. The votes of Marshall and Brennan, ordinarily cast in support of claims advanced by the accused and by the proponents of civil liberties, offset the Rehnquist-Burger alignment. The middle ground between the Rehnquist-Burger and Marshall-Brennan teams is occupied by Blackmun, Powell, White, Stewart, and Stevens. The votes of Blackmun and Powell reveal a discernible tilt toward the Rehnquist-Burger bloc, whereas those cast by Stevens disclose an affinity for the Marshall-Brennan bloc. Stewart and White seem to stand in mid field. A selected voting analysis of the Court's 1977–1978 term confirms this alignment of the justices.

Seventeen nonunanimous decisions regarding the administration of criminal justice were selected for review. Rehnquist supported the government on every occasion. Burger gave the government twelve favorable votes, Blackmum and Powell eleven and ten votes, respectively. White and Stewart each opposed the government on nine occasions, and Stevens favored the accused ten times. The liberal Marshall-Brennan bloc did not support the government in any of the seventeen cases.

The voting patterns in sixteen nonunanimous decisions regarding claims of civil rights and civil liberties were scrutinized. Rehnquist rebuffed these claims in every case and was joined by Burger fourteen times. Powell divided his sixteen votes evenly between rejecting and sustaining civil liberties claims and was followed closely by Blackmun, White, and Stewart who voted eight, nine, and nine times, respec-

Table 1

ACTION OF INDIVIDUAL JUSTICES

	Opinions Written[a]				Dissenting Votes[b] In Disposition By		
	Opinions of Court	Concur- rences	Dis- sents[c]	Total	Opinion	Memo- randum	Total
Blackmun	12	14	13	39	23	0	23
Brennan	13	7	13	33	38	10	48
Burger	16	6	7	29	30	2	32
Marshall	15	4	20	39	41	10	51
Powell	15	18	15	48	21	3	24
Rehnquist	14	7	24	45	41	5	46
Stevens	14	10	21	45	30	6	36
Stewart	15	10	13	38	20	2	22
White	15	5	17	37	28	6	34
Per curiam	6	—	—	6	—	—	—
Total	135	81	143	359	272	44	316

Note: A complete explanation of the way in which the tables are compiled may be found in "The Supreme Court, 1967 Term," *Harvard Law Review,* vol. 82 (1968), pp. 93, 301–2, and "The Supreme Court, 1969 Term," *Harvard Law Review,* vol. 84 (1970), pp. 30, 254–55.

Table 1, with the exception of the dissenting votes portion, deals only with full-opinion decisions disposing of cases on their merits. Six per curiam decisions were long enough to be considered full opinions. The memorandum tabulations include memorandum orders disposing of cases on the merits by affirming, reversing, vacating, or remanding. They exclude orders disposing of petitions for certiorari, dismissing writs of certiorari as improvidently granted, dismissing appeals for lack of jurisdiction or for lack of a substantial federal question, and disposing of miscellaneous applications. Certified questions are not included.

[a] A concurrence or dissent is recorded as a written opinion whenever a reason, however brief, is given, except when simply noted by the reporter.

[b] A justice is considered to have dissented when he voted to dispose of the case in any manner different from that of the majority of the Court.

[c] Opinions concurring in part and dissenting in part are counted as dissents.

Source: *Harvard Law Review,* vol. 92 (November 1978), p. 327, as corrected.

Table 2

DISPOSITION OF CASES: 1975, 1976, 1977 OCTOBER TERMS

Number of Cases	1975	1976	1977
Argued during term	179	176	172
Disposed of by full opinions	160	154	153
Disposed of by per curiam opinions	16	22	8
Set for reargument	3	0	9
Granted review during term	172	169	160
Total to be available for argument at outset of following term	99	88	75

Source: Office of the Clerk of the Supreme Court of the United States.

tively, in support of such claims. Stevens, Brennan, and Marshall generally endorsed assertions of civil liberties by voting 10–2, 9–2, and 13–2, respectively, to uphold their proponents.

1977–1978 Statistics

The caseload and output of the Supreme Court were marginally reduced from last term. The total number of cases on dockets declined from 4,730 to 4,704, while the number of cases acted upon fell from 4,104 to 3,950. The Court heard 172 cases argued, disposed of 153 by signed opinion, and decided 126 cases without oral argument. The corresponding figures for the 1976–1977 term were 176 cases argued, 154 disposed of by signed opinion, and 207 cases decided without oral argument.

2

SUMMARIES OF SIGNIFICANT DECISIONS

Criminal Law: Powers of the Police and Prosecutors

Two recurring issues of criminal law addressed by the Supreme Court during its 1977–1978 term were the permissibility of retrials under the double jeopardy clause of the Fifth Amendment and the propriety of various investigatory methods under federal statutes and the Fourth Amendment. Voicing doubts about its initial capacity to discern double jeopardy complexities in the wake of government appeals filed pursuant to the Criminal Appeals Act of 1970, the Court overruled a 1975 decision in the process of curtailing protections against double jeopardy. Double jeopardy jurisprudence remains in an unsettled state despite the Court's six significant attempts to search for transcendent principles to guide its development.

With a few important exceptions, the government's efforts to defend a variety of investigatory techniques ranging from the installation and operation of wiretaps to the use of warrants to search the premises of newspapers were vindicated by the Court. In addition, the Court continued to weaken the bite of the exclusionary ruling that prohibits exploitation by the government in criminal cases of evidence seized unconstitutionally. The government was rebuffed, however, in seeking constitutional endorsement for warrantless searches of murder scenes or of the working areas of business premises.

Since an overwhelming percentage of criminal cases is disposed of through plea bargaining, rulings that affect the bargaining leverage of either the prosecutor or the accused are of enormous practical significance. The negotiating position of the prosecutor was strengthened this term in a decision that conferred constitutional blessing on threats by prosecutors to reindict an accused for more serious offenses if he declined to plead guilty to lesser charges.

Double Jeopardy. The spirit of Fifth Amendment protection against double jeopardy was elegantly stated in *Green* v. *United States,* 355 U.S. 184, 187 (1957):

> The underlying idea, one that is deeply ingrained in at least the Anglo-American system of jurisprudence, is that the State with all its resources and power should not be allowed to make repeated attempts to convict an individual for an alleged offense, thereby subjecting him to embarrassment, expense and ordeal and compelling him to live in a continuing state of anxiety and insecurity, as well as enhancing the possibility that even though innocent he may be found guilty.

The Court has repeatedly acknowledged, however, that compelling interests of law enforcement may require subordination of these double jeopardy values and can justify retrials of defendants in a variety of circumstances. The Court struggled this term to explain when government appeals or retrials in criminal cases would be inoffensive to Fifth Amendment safeguards.

In *United States* v. *Scott,* 437 U.S. 82 (1978), the defendant moved before his trial and twice during it to dismiss two counts of an indictment on the ground that preindictment delay had unconstitutionally prejudiced his defense. At the close of the evidence the motion was granted, and the government sought to appeal to the court of appeals. That court dismissed the appeal, holding that any further prosecution of the defendant was barred by the double jeopardy clause as construed in *United States* v. *Jenkins,* 420 U.S. 358 (1975). Reversing by a 5–4 vote and overruling *Jenkins,* the Court concluded that a defendant who seeks termination of a criminal proceeding on a basis "unrelated to factual guilt or innocence of the offense of which he is accused" lacks any double jeopardy protection against an appeal by the government of a trial court decision in his favor. *Jenkins* had held that double jeopardy norms could not countenance government appeals in circumstances in which "further proceedings of some sort, devoted to the resolution of factual issues going to the elements of the offense charged," would be required upon reversal and remand.

The Court's attempt to distinguish between dismissals founded on a determination of factual innocence, which are constitutionally shielded from appeal, and those that are not, which can be appealed, seemed cryptic at best. It stated that dismissals or acquittals founded on the defenses of insanity and entrapment stem from factual findings that the accused lacked criminal culpability and thus fall into the former category, whereas dismissals resting on preindictment delays may be appealed because they represent legal conclusions that de-

21

fendants, although criminally culpable, may not be punished because of supposed constitutional violations.

At issue in *Arizona* v. *Washington*, 434 U.S. 497 (1978), was a double jeopardy attack on a retrial after improper and prejudicial comments contained in the opening statement of the defense counsel had triggered a mistrial. Finding no constitutional infirmity in the retrial, the Court explained that the prejudicial statement had irreparably biased the jurors against the government and was an insurmountable obstacle to a just verdict. The public interest in the impartial administration of justice, the Court stated, must prevail over a defendant's interest in being tried by the first jury impaneled.

Double jeopardy claims were embraced sympathetically in *Burks* v. *United States*, 437 U.S. 1 (1978), and *Sanabria* v. *United States*, 437 U.S. 54 (1978). In the former, the Court concluded by an 8–0 vote that double jeopardy values will not tolerate the reprosecution of a defendant after a jury verdict of guilty has been properly overturned by a court on the ground that the evidence was insufficient to support the verdict. A retrial, the Court declared, would offer the government an unfair opportunity to close the gaps in its evidence. The Court also observed that a defendant does not forfeit his double jeopardy protection against retrial simply because he requests a new trial rather than an acquittal as a remedy for flaws in the evidence that led to a verdict of guilty.

In *Sanabria*, a 7–2 majority held that a defendant was protected against retrial after a midtrial acquittal, which stemmed from legally erroneous rulings, was granted by a trial judge. The rulings led the judge to conclude that evidence of guilt was insufficient as a matter of law. The Court refused the government's invitation to create an exception to the double jeopardy teaching that an acquittal bars a retrial no matter how egregiously erroneous the legal rulings that led to that judgment might be. The *Scott* decision, however, endorsed retrials if the acquittal is founded on a basis unrelated to factual guilt or innocence.

The double jeopardy clause was also invoked as an insurmountable barrier to retrial in *Crist* v. *Bretz*, 437 U.S. 28 (1978). After a jury had been impaneled and sworn, but before the first witness was called, a state court granted the prosecutor's motion to dismiss in order to permit the filing of amended information that would correct inaccurate statements alleged in the initial charges. Defending the constitutionality of a retrial, the state argued that a defendant is not placed in jeopardy until the first witness testifies. The Court ruled, however, that in both federal and state courts, jeopardy attaches when the jury has been impaneled and sworn.

In *Swisher* v. *Brady*, 438 U.S. 204 (1978), no double jeopardy infirmity was found in a two-tier juvenile court system that empowered court masters to make *proposed* findings and recommendations on charges of juvenile delinquency, while placing *final* authority to accept, reject, or modify the recommendations in juvenile judges. Under the contested procedures, a complete evidentiary record is ordinarily built before the master. The state may challenge a proposed finding of nondelinquency before a juvenile judge, but no additional evidence may be submitted without the consent of the minor. In light of the advisory nature of the master's powers, the Court was unpersuaded by the argument that their recommendations of nondelinquency were tantamount to acquittals and that permitting rejection of the recommendations by juvenile judges was irreconcilable with the doctrine of double jeopardy.

Government Powers of Investigation: Searches, Seizures, and Inspections. The Fourth Amendment condemns warrantless searches and seizures, subject only to a few specific, well-delineated exceptions. In a trilogy of decisions this term, the Court expounded on the scope of these exceptions and generally resisted government efforts to increase their number.

In *Mincey* v. *Arizona*, 437 U.S. 385 (1978), a state unsuccessfully urged the Court to embrace an exception to the warrant requirement with respect to search of the scene of a murder. It was contended that the strong government interest in solving crimes of murder could justify warrantless searches at any time on premises where homicides had occurred. Emphasizing that the Fourth Amendment embraces privacy values that cannot be discarded simply to increase the effectiveness of law enforcement, the Court refused to eviscerate constitutional safeguards to help solve serious crime. It did note, however, that a threatened or actual homicide may create emergencies that justify warrantless searches for limited times and purposes. Police may make warrantless entries and searches of premises, the Court stated, when they have reason to believe that a person within is in need of immediate aid. And when the police arrive at the scene of a homicide, the Court continued, the Fourth Amendment is no barrier to a prompt warrantless search of the area for possible additional victims or the killer.

Warrantless searches to discover the origins of a fire in a commercial store were challenged in *Michigan* v. *Tyler*, 436 U.S. 499 (1978). Convicted of conspiracy to burn real property, defendants argued that the warrantless searches of the burned premises violated Fourth Amendment safeguards against overzealous investigation. Writing for the Court, Justice Stewart spelled out the governing principles for determining whether a warrantless search to discover the origins of a fire passes constitutional muster. As a general matter, he stated, official entries to discover the cause of a fire—not evidence of crime— can be justified only by a warrant. Because such searches lack criminal focus, however, warrants issued in accordance with reasonable legislative, administrative, or judicial standards, but lacking probable cause, are sufficient to satisfy the Fourth Amendment. Stewart noted, however, that a burning building creates an exigency of sufficient gravity to justify a warrantless entry to extinguish the blaze and warrantless searches for a reasonable time thereafter to discover clues as to the origins of the fire. Finally, Stewart explained, if while lawfully searching for the cause of a blaze investigators discover probable cause to believe that a crime has occurred, further access to the premises to gather evidence for a possible prosecution must be justified by a warrant founded on probable cause.

In *Marshall* v. *Barlow's Inc.*, 436 U.S. 307 (1978), the Court expressed some hostility toward warrantless administrative searches that had been endorsed with respect to the heavily regulated liquor and firearms industries in *Colonnade Catering Corporation* v. *United States*, 397 U.S. 72 (1970), and *United States* v. *Biswell*, 406 U.S. 311 (1972). At issue in *Barlow* was the constitutionality of a statute that empowered investigators to make warrantless entries into the working areas of businesses to search for noncriminal violations of the Occupational Safety and Health Act (OSHA). While holding that the statute offended the general warrant clause of the Fourth Amendment, the Court largely vitiated the enforcement significance of the decision by refusing to make a showing of probable cause to believe that an employer's premises contained a violation of the OSHA, a condition of issuance of a warrant under the act. It stated:

> A warrant showing that a specific business has been chosen for an OSHA search on the basis of a general administrative plan for the enforcement of the Act derived from neutral sources such as, for example, dispersion of employees in various types of industries across a given area, and the desired frequency of searches in any of the lesser divisions of the area, would protect an employer's Fourth Amendment rights.

The ordinary motorist suffered a Fourth Amendment setback in *Pennsylvania* v. *Mimms*, 434 U.S. 106 (1977). Voicing concern about the number of police killed after stopping traffic violators, the Court held that officers could compel such offenders to get out of their cars irrespective of articulatable threats to police safety or suspicion that criminal activity was afoot. The police also garnered a significant victory in *Zurcher* v. *Stanford Daily*, 436 U.S. 547 (1978), which held that neither the press nor other innocent persons enjoy any special Fourth Amendment shelter against warrants authorizing searches for evidence of crime committed by third parties.

The Burger Court has displayed unrelenting hostility to the Fourth Amendment's exclusionary rule that generally prohibits the use of unconstitutionally seized evidence in criminal cases.[1] No retreat from this attitude was evident in *United States* v. *Ceccolini*, 435 U.S. 268 (1978), where the Court circumscribed the so-called fruits-of-the-poisonous-tree doctrine. As explained in *Wong Sun* v. *United States*, 371 U.S. 471 (1963), the doctrine bans the use in a criminal case of evidence that has been obtained as the fruit of a Fourth Amendment violation unless the tie between the lawless conduct and the challenged evidence is "so attenuated as to dissipate the taint." *Ceccolini* declared that when a cooperative witness is discovered in the wake of a constitutional infraction, suppression of the witness's testimony under the exclusionary rule is disfavored. This conclusion, the Court asserted, is justified because cooperative witnesses would probably have volunteered their aid. Investigators, therefore, have little incentive to commit constitutional violations to discover the identities or whereabouts of these witnesses.

The government warded off attacks on the exercise of statutory powers of investigation in *United States* v. *New York Telephone Co.*, 434 U.S. 159 (1977), and *Scott* v. *United States*, 436 U.S. 128 (1978). In the former case, the Court held that the All Writs Act empowered a federal district court to order a telephone company to offer federal law enforcement officials the facilities and technical assistance necessary to install a properly authorized pen register on a telephone suspected of facilitating criminal conduct. (A pen register is a mechanical device that records the numbers dialed on a telephone but neither intercepts communications nor discloses whether calls are completed.)

In *Scott*, the government's operation of a wiretap under the Omnibus Crime Control and Safe Streets Act was questioned. One pro-

---

[1] See, for example, Stone v. Powell, 428 U.S. 465 (1976) (circumscribing the scope of habeas corpus review of Fourth Amendment claims); United States v. Janis, 428 U.S. 433 (1976) (declining to apply exclusionary rule to bar the use of evidence unconstitutionally seized by state officers in a civil proceeding by or against the United States); United States v. Peltier, 422 U.S. 531 (1975) (refusing retroactive application of the exclusionary rule); United States v. Calandra, 414 U.S. 338 (1974) (declining to apply exclusionary rule to grand jury proceedings).

vision of the act is a requirement that wiretapping be conducted in such a way as to minimize the interception of innocent conversations. A district court condemned indiscriminate wiretap interceptions of conversations over a particular phone for a period of one month because the listening agents had made no attempt to minimize the seizure of innocent calls. Declaring that the district court had erred, the Supreme Court held that the minimization demands of the act are satisfied if interceptions of innocent conversations are reasonable when viewed objectively in the light of all the circumstances. In making this determination, the Court said, the percentage and duration of nonpertinent calls intercepted, the nature of the crime under investigation, and the type of use to which the telephone is normally put are all relevant. The act was not offended, the Court concluded, simply because agents intentionally failed to seek to minimize the interception of innocent calls.

Plea Bargaining. The ability of prosecutors to negotiate pleas of guilty to their satisfaction was enhanced as a consequence of *Bordenkircher* v. *Hayes*, 434 U.S. 357 (1978). There the Court found no due process infirmity in vindicating a threat to reindict the accused for a more serious crime if he refused to accept a proposed plea agreement. Writing for a 5–4 majority, Justice Stewart concluded that to condemn such threats when an enhanced charge is legally justified would do violence to the "very premises that underlie the concept of plea bargaining itself."

United States v. *Scott,* 437 U.S. 82 (1978)

Facts: In *United States* v. *Jenkins,* 420 U.S. 358 (1975), the Court held that a trial court's dismissal of an indictment after jeopardy had attached was shielded from appellate review by the double jeopardy clause if "further proceedings of some sort, devoted to the resolution of factual issues going to the elements of the offense charged," would be required upon reversal and remand. Relying on *Jenkins,* a court of appeals held that the double jeopardy clause precluded a government appeal of a mid-trial dismissal of an indictment for prejudicial preindictment delay.

Question: Should *Jenkins* be overruled and the government appeal permitted on the issue of prejudicial preindictment delay?

Decision: Yes. Opinion by Justice Rehnquist. Vote: 5–4, Brennan, White, Marshall, and Stevens dissenting.

Reasons: Until 1971, statutory restraints on the right of the government to appeal in federal criminal cases generally shielded the Court from exposure to the multiple subtleties of the double jeopardy clause. *Jenkins* represented a pioneering effort to grapple with the double jeopardy contentions unlocked by the Criminal Appeals Act, 18 U.S. Code 3731, which authorizes government appeals unless the double jeopardy clause would prohibit further prosecution. The vastly increased exposure of the Court to double jeopardy claims since *Jenkins* has revealed the flaws in the reasoning underlying that decision.

> It placed an unwarrantedly great emphasis on the defendant's right to have his guilt decided by the first jury empaneled to try him so as to include those cases where the defendant himself seeks to terminate the trial before verdict on grounds unrelated to factual guilt or innocence.

The guiding principle of the double jeopardy clause is that the government "with all its resources and power should not be allowed to make repeated attempts to convict an individual for an alleged offense, thereby subjecting him to embarrassment, expense and ordeal and compelling him to live in a continuing state of anxiety and insecurity." A bulwark against government oppression, this principle is not offended by a retrial after a defendant has managed to abort an initial trial on grounds unrelated to guilt or innocence. In such cases, the retrial is not the offspring of government overreaching but of the defendant's election to forestall a verdict on his alleged criminal culpability.

When an accused obtains a dismissal founded on the insufficiency of the government's evidence to rebut legal defenses for otherwise criminal acts—such as insanity or entrapment—then *Burks* v. *United States*, 437 U.S. 1 (1978), forecloses any government appeal. But the double jeopardy clause is no obstacle to government appeals of dismissals founded on a "legal judgment that a defendant, although criminally culpable, may not be punished because of a supposed constitutional violation." Because a dismissal for preindictment delay falls into the latter category, the government may challenge the correctness of such legal rulings on appeal. This doctrine of double jeopardy will significantly advance the public interest in the resolution of criminal cases on their merits without enhancing the possibility that innocent persons may be found guilty.

27

Arizona v. *Washington,* 434 U.S. 497 (1978)

Facts: During his opening statement, defense counsel improperly informed the jury that his client had previously been granted a new trial because of the prosecutor's misconduct. That evidence would have been inadmissible at trial as irrelevant to the issue of guilt or innocence. The prosecutor's motion for a mistrial was initially denied, then renewed after two witnesses had testified. The motion was granted without an express finding by the trial judge that there was "manifest necessity" for a mistrial because defense counsel's improper remarks had engendered incurable prejudice in the jury. The accused then obtained federal habeas corpus relief barring a retrial on the ground that it would offend the double jeopardy clause of the Fifth Amendment. A federal court of appeals ruled that the clause shields an accused from retrial when a mistrial is declared at the behest of the government without a finding of manifest necessity or an explicit consideration of alternative remedies that might assure a fair and impartial verdict.

Question: Was the trial judge's declaration of a mistrial without an express finding of manifest necessity or explicit consideration of alternatives fatal to a retrial under the double jeopardy clause?

Decision: No. Opinion by Justice Stevens. Vote: 6–3, Blackmun concurring, White, Marshall, and Brennan dissenting.

Reasons: The double jeopardy clause protects an accused against dual prosecutions for the same offense. The protection has been scrupulously safeguarded because a second prosecution "increases the financial and emotional burden on the accused, prolongs the period in which he is stigmatized by an unresolved accusation of wrongdoing, and may even enhance the risk that an innocent defendant may be convicted." It is well established, nevertheless, that double jeopardy jurisprudence is not blind to the interest of the community in obtaining public justice. A mistrial founded on manifest necessity and declared over the objection of the accused does not bar a retrial. Manifest necessity may exist where actions not attributable to the prosecutor or judge seriously threaten the impartiality of the jury. Although the potential for bias may be difficult to predict, "the overriding interest in the evenhanded administration of justice requires that we accord the highest degree of respect to the trial judge's evaluation of the likelihood that the impartiality of one or more jurors may have been affected by [an] improper comment."

In this case, defense counsel exposed the jury to improper and highly prejudicial evidence. Before granting a mistrial, the trial judge carefully weighed the interest of the accused in a single trial against the probable bias of the jury caused by the impropriety. The order did not exceed the discretion permitted by the double jeopardy clause and was clearly intended to vindicate the public interest in fair trials and impartial verdicts. So long as the record supplies a sufficient justification for a mistrial, it cannot be disturbed simply because there was no express finding of manifest necessity or articulation of all the factors underlying the decision.

Burks v. *United States*, 437 U.S. 1 (1978)

Facts: After a jury verdict of guilty, a defendant moved for a new trial, claiming that the evidence was insufficient to rebut his proof with respect to insanity. The district court denied the motion, but the court of appeals reversed, holding that the government had failed to discharge its burden of proving sanity beyond a reasonable doubt. Rather than order a directed verdict of acquittal, however, the court of appeals remanded the case to the district court to determine whether a directed verdict of acquittal should be entered or a new trial ordered. Seeking review of the remand order, the defendant contended that a retrial would offend the double jeopardy clause.

Question: Does the double jeopardy clause of the Fifth Amendment foreclose the possibility of a retrial when an appellate court overturns a conviction solely for lack of sufficient evidence to sustain the jury's verdict?

Decision: Yes. Opinion by Chief Justice Burger. Vote: 8–0. Blackmun did not participate.

Reasons: Prior decisions expounding the double jeopardy clause lend support to the view that a defendant who requests a new trial on appeal may be subject to retrial, even when his conviction is reversed for insufficiency of the evidence. These cases, however, erroneously failed to distinguish between reversals that are the result of trial error and those that are the result of insufficient evidence. In cases of the former type, reversal implies nothing with respect to the defendant's guilt or innocence. A retrial is permitted in such circumstances because of the strong interest of the community in punishing the guilty. A reversal of the latter type, however, is tantamount to a jury verdict of not guilty. It reflects a legal determination that the government failed to shoulder its burden of proof despite a fair opportunity to present whatever evidence of guilt it could assemble. A jury verdict of acquittal—no matter how erroneous—is beyond government challenge; society has no "greater interest in retrying a defendant when, on review, it is decided as a matter of law that the jury could not properly have returned a verdict of guilty."

Accordingly, the double jeopardy clause shields a defendant from retrial once an appellate court has found the evidence of guilt legally insufficient. A judgment of acquittal is the only just remedy in such cases, whether or not the defendant has requested a new trial. A motion for a new trial does not constitute a waiver of the right to an acquittal.

Sanabria v. United States, 437 U.S. 54 (1978)

Facts: Sanabria was indicted, along with several others, for violating 18 U.S. Code 1955, which makes it a federal offense to participate in the operation of an "illegal gambling business." The indictment charged that Sanabria had participated in an illegal gambling business that was engaged in horsebetting and numbers betting in violation of Massachusetts law. At the close of the evidence, but before submission of the case to the jury, the district court erroneously ruled that the indictment improperly alleged unlawful numbers betting and thus struck all evidence relating to that conduct. It then granted Sanabria's motion for a judgment of acquittal because of insufficient evidence tying him to horsebetting activities.

Seeking a new trial on the portion of the indictment related to numbers betting, the government appealed the decision to exclude evidence and enter a judgment of acquittal. Reversing the district court and granting the requested relief, the court of appeals held that the double jeopardy clause did not shield Sanabria from a retrial.

Question: Does the double jeopardy clause of the Fifth Amendment bar a retrial of Sanabria?

Decision: Yes. Opinion by Justice Marshall. Vote: 7–2, White concurring in part, Blackmun and Rehnquist dissenting.

Reasons: The primary purpose of the double jeopardy clause is to prevent successive trials. It is fundamental to double jeopardy jurisprudence that an acquittal, even when founded on an erroneous legal interpretation, forecloses the possibility of a new trial for the same offense.

The government urges that Sanabria was acquitted of the portion of the section 1955 count related to horsebetting, but not of that portion related to numbers betting. The district court's acquittal order, however, went to the entire count, even though it stemmed from an erroneous ruling on the evidence related to numbers betting. Even if the acquittal was related only to the horsebetting allegation, moreover, a retrial on the numbers allegation would offend the double jeopardy clause. The indictment charged Sanabria with participation in a single gambling business, albeit with horsebetting and numbers betting offshoots. His acquittal was founded on insufficient proof of connection with this business. A subsequent trial of Sanabria for participation in the same gambling business would expose him to a second trial for the same offense of which he was acquitted.

Although Sanabria's acquittal was grounded on the erroneous exclusion of evidence related to numbers betting, the double jeopardy clause shields it from challenge on appeal. This safeguard against successive trials is not forfeited simply because the legal error was induced by a motion of the accused. A different question would be presented if an accused, afforded an opportunity to obtain a pretrial ruling on the merits of a legal defense, nevertheless knowingly permitted his exposure to jeopardy before raising the defense.

Crist v. *Bretz*, 437 U.S. 28 (1978)

Facts: After a jury had been selected and sworn but before the first witness was called, a state trial court dismissed an information charging the defendants with false pretenses and related crimes because of a typographical error in specifying the date on which their illegal conduct had begun. After a corrected information had been filed, the defendants were tried and convicted. Affirming the convictions, the Montana Supreme Court rejected the contention that the double jeopardy clause of the Fifth Amendment barred prosecution of the defendants under the second information. Jeopardy does not attach under state law, the court noted, until the first witness is sworn. Accordingly, it held that the defendants had not been placed in jeopardy in the aborted initial trial.

A federal court of appeals granted the defendants habeas corpus relief, reasoning that the constitutional protection against double jeopardy compels adherence to the rule in both state and federal prosecutions that jeopardy attaches when a jury is impaneled and sworn. It thus held that the double jeopardy clause invalidated the contested convictions.

Question: Does the double jeopardy clause of the Fifth Amendment require both state and federal courts to embrace the rule that jeopardy attaches in jury trials when the jury is sworn?

Decision: Yes. Opinion by Justice Stewart. Vote: 6–3, Powell, Burger, and Rennquist dissenting.

Reasons: In *Downum* v. *United States,* 372 U.S. 734 (1963), the Court implicitly acknowledged that jeopardy attaches in federal jury trials after a jury has been sworn. This rule vindicates a defendant's powerful interest in retaining a particular jury to determine his guilt or innocence. It is integral to concerns of double jeopardy—"the finality of judgments, the minimization of harassing exposure to the harrowing experience of a criminal trial, and the valued right to continue with the chosen jury"—and its application is thus required in both state and federal prosecutions.

Swisher v. *Brady,* 438 U.S. 204 (1978)

Facts: Maryland law provides for a bifurcated proceeding to adjudicate juvenile offenses. In the first stage, a master holds a hearing and proposes findings, conclusions, recommendations, or orders to a juvenile court judge. At the second stage, the state and the accused may file exceptions to the master's proposals, additional evidence may be adduced before the judge if no party objects, and the judge accepts, rejects, or modifies the master's proposals. Juveniles involved in proceedings in which the state had filed exceptions to a master's proposed findings of nondelinquency brought suit in a federal district court contending that the double jeopardy clause proscribed any departure from the recommendations by a juvenile court judge. The district court agreed.

Question: Does Maryland's bifurcated procedure for adjudicating juvenile delinquency offenses contravene the double jeopardy clause of the Fifth Amendment?

Decision: No. Opinion by Chief Justice Burger. Vote: 6–3, Marshall, Brennan, and Powell dissenting.

Reasons: The double jeopardy clause prohibits a state's exposing an accused to successive trials for the same offense. A central purpose of the prohibition is to deny the state an opportunity to cure the shortcomings of its evidence in the first proceeding. Another purpose is to reduce the risk that an innocent person will be convicted. This is achieved by insulating from appeal by the government a final judgment of acquittal that rests on factual innocence. These dual double jeopardy concerns are not offended by Maryland's bifurcated procedure for adjudicating juvenile delinquency offenses. If the state files exceptions to a master's proposed finding of nondelinquency, it may not offer additional evidence unless the accused consents. In addition, a proposed finding of nondelinquency is not a final judgment; the juvenile court judge retains exclusive power to make findings and render final judgments of acquittal or conviction. To the extent that the judge supplements the findings of those proposed by the master—either on his own initiative or at the behest of the state or the accused—he does so without exposing the accused to a second trial or offending the double jeopardy clause.

Mincey v. Arizona, 437 U.S. 385 (1978)

Facts: During a narcotics raid conducted by several policemen at Mincey's apartment, a volley of bullets left one policeman dead and Mincey seriously wounded. After the shooting, homicide detectives searched the apartment exhaustively for four days without obtaining a warrant. In addition, Mincey was interrogated by a police detective about the incident while in the intensive care unit of a hospital and in disregard of several requests that interrogation cease until he had retained a lawyer. He was ultimately convicted of narcotics offenses through the use of evidence seized during the warrantless searches and statements made in response to the police interrogation. Affirming the convictions, the Arizona Supreme Court held that a warrantless search of the scene of a homicide does not offend the Fourth Amendment and that Mincey's statements were voluntary and thus constitutionally admissible.

Questions: (1) Are searches of the scenes of homicides exempted from the general Fourth Amendment warrant requirement? (2) Were the statements made by Mincey during the interrogation in the hospital involuntary and thus constitutionally tainted if used for any purpose during his trial?

Decision: No to the first question and yes to the second. Opinion by Justice Stewart. Votes: 9–0 and 8–1 respectively, Rehnquist dissenting in part.

Reasons: It is a cardinal principle of Fourth Amendment jurisprudence that warrantless searches are impermissible per se, subject to a few specifically established, well-delineated exceptions. These exceptions have generally been embraced when reasonable needs of law enforcement could be seriously impaired if a warrant were required. This rationale, however, offers no justification for a wholesale exception to the requirement of a warrant for any search of the scene of a homicide. In this case, for example, the four-day warrantless search of Mincey's apartment was not necessary to forestall an imminent threat to life or limb or the destruction or removal of evidence. And the mere fact that the investigation of serious crimes would be made more efficient can never by itself justify disregard of the Fourth Amendment. Although police may conduct a prompt warrantless search of the scene of a homicide for other possible victims or for the killer, there is no blanket murder-scene exception to the Fourth Amendment requirement of a warrant.

The statements made by Mincey during his interrogation while in the hospital were used solely for the purposes of impeachment at trial. This limited use, nevertheless, would offend due process if the statements were involuntary—that is, not the product of a free and rational will. Numerous factors compel a finding of involuntariness. The statements were made while Mincey was in extreme pain, encumbered by tubes, needles, and breathing apparatus, and on the edge of consciousness. Several responses were wholly uninformative, confirmed Mincey's assertions that he could not think clearly, and were made after entreaties that he be left alone had been ignored. In sum, the statements were the product of an overborne will, whose use in any way at Mincey's trial was condemned by due process.

Michigan v. *Tyler*, 436 U.S. 499 (1978)

Facts: Shortly before midnight on January 21, 1970, a fire broke out at a furniture store. During the ensuing four hours, firefighters, police, and fire officials entered the burning premises without warrants to extinguish the blaze and discover its origins. A search of the gutted store revealed evidence of arson. At 4:00 A.M., after the fire had been extinguished, the store was temporarily vacated for four hours, after which fire and police inspectors returned to search for additional clues to its cause. They discovered further evidence of arson. Several weeks later, a police arson investigator again conducted a warrantless search of the store that confirmed arson as the cause of the fire. Thereafter, the lessee of the store and his business associate were convicted of conspiracy to burn real property in violation of Michigan law. The trial judge rejected their contention that the Fourth Amendment required suppression of the evidence obtained by police and fire officials through warrantless searches of the burned store after the fire had been extinguished. Reversing the convictions, the Michigan Supreme Court held that fidelity to the Fourth Amendment requires that police and fire officials obtain warrants to enter and search burned premises once the blaze has been extinguished and firefighters have ended their work, absent consent or abandonment of the premises.

Question: Were the warrantless entries and searches of the burned furniture store constitutionally infirm under the Fourth Amendment?

Decision: Only the entry and search conducted several weeks after the fire was constitutionally tainted. Opinion by Justice Stewart. Vote: 7–1, Rehnquist dissenting. Brennan did not participate.

Reasons: Fourth Amendment safeguards against arbitrary government invasions of privacy protect commercial buildings and circumscribe the authority of criminal, civil, or administrative investigators. An occupant of burned premises is not stripped of these safeguards simply because he is ordinarily an innocent victim and often must vacate the premises. Victims of a fire retain a legitimate expectation of privacy regarding personal effects and portions of the premises that are habitable. Accordingly, entries and searches of fire-damaged premises must be justified by warrants absent exigent circumstances that render warrantless entries or searches reasonable under the Fourth Amendment.

A warrant authorizing entry to investigate the cause of a fire, however, may be issued without a demonstration of probable cause to believe that evidence of wrongdoing or crime will be discovered. A showing that the investigation is the offspring of reasonable standards will justify issuance of the warrant. But once a search to discover the cause of a fire has been transformed into a criminal investigation, probable cause must be shown to obtain warrants to justify further access for the purpose of gathering evidence for a possible prosecution.

In this case, exigent circumstances justified the initial warrantless entries and searches of the furniture store. A burning building may be entered by firefighters, and evidence of arson in plain view may be seized without offending the Fourth Amendment. Since fire officials are charged with determining the origin of a fire and forestalling any recurrence, moreover, they may remain in a burned building for a reasonable time after the blaze has been extinguished to preserve evidence and to search for continuing danger. The delay engendered by requiring a warrant for such inspections would frequently frustrate their purposes.

Here the warrantless entry and search of the furniture store a mere four hours after the blaze had been extinguished was tantamount to a continuation of the initial valid entry and search; accordingly, the lack of a warrant did not taint the resulting seizure of evidence. The warrantless entry and search conducted several weeks after the fire, however, was clearly detached from the initial exigency and therefore was proscribed by the Fourth Amendment.

Marshall v. *Barlow's Inc.,* 436 U.S. 307 (1978)

Facts: Section 8(a) of the Occupational Safety and Health Act (OSHA) of 1970 empowers agents of the secretary of labor to conduct warrantless searches of an employer's work area to uncover safety hazards and violations of OSHA regulations. Having refused an OSHA inspector warrantless entry onto the premises of his business, an employer brought suit attacking section 8(a) as a violation of the Fourth Amendment. Sustaining the attack, a three-judge federal district court ruled that warrantless inspections authorized by section 8(a) overstepped the Fourth Amendment safeguards against unreasonable searches.

Question: Do warrantless inspections conducted pursuant to section 8(a) violate the Fourth Amendment?

Decision: Yes. Opinion by Justice White. Vote: 5–3, Stevens, Blackmun, and Rehnquist dissenting. Brennan did not participate.

Reasons: A primary spur to the adoption of the Fourth Amendment was the colonists' revulsion against writs of assistance that conferred sweeping power on customs officials and other royal agents to search business premises in order to exact compliance with revenue measures and to discover smuggled goods. Accordingly, it would be untenable to deny the general protection of the Fourth Amendment against warrantless searches to places of business. This protection restrains government agents during civil as well as criminal investigations.

The Court has carved out exceptions to the warrant requirement, however, for pervasively regulated industries, such as liquor and firearms, where companies are stripped of any expectation of privacy from government oversight. This rationale is inapplicable to businesses subject to the OSHA because detailed federal regulation of the working conditions of employees is of recent vintage and virtually no employer can escape its grasp.

Warrantless searches may also survive Fourth Amendment scrutiny if a weighing of administrative necessity against threatened invasions of privacy makes them reasonable. Here the secretary's regulations belie the assertion that warrantless inspections are necessary to effective enforcement of the OSHA. They oblige inspectors to enlist judicial process if an employer denies them entry. Warrants will not foreclose the possibility of surprise visits, moreover, because they may be issued *ex parte* and executed without delay or prior notice to the employer. Finally, a warrant to inspect for a violation of the OSHA may be issued without demonstrating probable cause. Generally speaking, administrative searches may be justified by warrants based only on a showing that reasonable legislative or administrative standards for conducting an inspection are satisfied with respect to a particular establishment. Therefore,

> [a] warrant showing that a specific business has been chosen for an OSHA search on the basis of a general administrative plan for the enforcement of the Act derived from neutral sources such as, for example, dispersion of employees in various types of industries across a given area, and the desired frequency of searches in any of the lesser divisions of the area, would protect an employer's Fourth Amendment rights.

Conditioning OSHA inspections on warrants will protect substantial values of privacy by curtailing the discretion of agents as to when and where to search and whom to search. The Fourth Amendment cannot countenance subordinating this protection to the insignificant contribution to enforcement of the OSHA offered by warrantless inspections.

Pennsylvania v. *Mimms,* 434 U.S. 106 (1977)

Facts: Observing Mimms driving an automobile with an expired license plate, two police officers stopped the vehicle to issue a traffic summons. Mimms was ordered to step out of the car and produce his owner's card and operator's license. Obeying the policemen's request, Mimms was frisked for weapons by an officer who had noticed a large bulge under his sports jacket. The officer discovered a revolver, a discovery that led to Mimms's conviction for unlawfully carrying an unlicensed firearm. The Pennsylvania Supreme Court overturned the conviction on the ground that the order to Mimms to get out of the car violated the Fourth Amendment protection against unreasonable seizures. It concluded that a constitutional foundation for such orders can be claimed only if there are objectively observable facts to support a suspicion that criminal activity is afoot or that the occupants of the vehicle pose a threat to the safety of the police.

Question: When the driver of a vehicle is properly stopped for a traffic violation, does the Fourth Amendment prohibit the police from ordering the driver out of the car absent particularized suspicion that he threatens police safety?

Decision: No. Per curiam opinion. Vote: 6-3, Brennan, Marshall, and Stevens dissenting.

Reasons: The reasonableness of searches and seizures under the Fourth Amendment depends on a balance between the public interest at stake and the individual's right to personal security, free from arbitrary interference by the government. Permitting police to order occupants of vehicles out of their cars diminishes the possibility of assaults on law enforcement personnel. A driver may use a car as a shield to make unobserved movements, and in one study it was revealed that a substantial percentage of police shootings occur when a suspect seated in an automobile is approached. Additionally, requiring an officer to converse with a traffic violator while standing alongside the car increases the risk of accidental injury from passing vehicles. In contrast, a driver whose vehicle has been legitimately stopped suffers only a *de minimus* intrusion on personal liberty when ordered out of the car. Hardly rising to the level of a petty indignity, this intrusion must yield to the legitimate concerns for an officer's safety.

United States v. Ceccolini, 435 U.S. 268 (1978)

Facts: In December 1974, a uniformed police officer entered a flower shop and conversed with Lois Hennessey, an employee. During the conversation, the officer spotted an envelope containing money on a cash register, seized it, and discovered policy slips inside. Returning the envelope, the officer asked Hennessey to whom it belonged and was informed that it was Ceccolini's. This information was transmitted to an FBI agent, who interviewed Hennessey four months later regarding knowledge of Ceccolini's activities that she had acquired as an employee of the flower shop. Thereafter, a federal indictment for perjury was returned against Ceccolini in which it was charged that his testimony before a grand jury in which he denied that he had taken policy bets at the flower shop was false. After trial, the district court concluded that Hennessey's testimony should have been suppressed because it was obtained as a product of the unconstitutional search of the envelope. Without her testimony, there was insufficient evidence to justify the verdict of guilty that had been conditionally entered pending a ruling on Ceccolini's motion to suppress. The court of appeals affirmed.

Question: Should Hennessey's trial testimony have been suppressed as a product of the unconstitutional search of the envelope in the flower shop?

Decision: No. Opinion by Justice Rehnquist. Vote: 6–2, Burger concurring in the judgment, Marshall and Brennan dissenting. Blackmun did not participate.

Reasons: In *Wong Sun* v. *United States,* 371 U.S. 471 (1963), the Court concluded that evidence come upon as a consequence of a Fourth Amendment violation is untainted once its link to the unconstitutional conduct has become sufficiently attenuated. The line of attenuation should be drawn by weighing the deterrent value of excluding the evidence at issue against the public interest in having convictions or acquittals founded on reliable evidence. With regard to a live witness, the greater the duration between the initial illegality and the testimony alleged to be tainted and the greater the willingness of the witness to cooperate and testify freely, the stronger the case for admitting the testimony. In addition, an exclusion order "would perpetually disable a witness from testifying about relevant and material facts, regardless of how unrelated such testimony might be to the purpose of the originally illegal search or the evidence discovered thereby." This enhanced threat to reliable verdicts engendered by suppressing the testimony of a live witness requires that it be more directly linked to the initial illegality than other types of evidence before its use is condemned under the Fourth Amendment.

Under the guidance of these principles, the Court concludes that the line of attenuation had been crossed when Hennessey's testimony was obtained. It was given freely and lacked any connection to the unconstitutional discovery of the policy slips in the envelope. Considerable time elapsed between the initial contact with Hennessey by the FBI and her testimony at the trial. Even apart from knowledge of the policy slips, Hennessey's general relationship with Ceccolini was well known to investigators. Finally, there is no evidence to suggest that the illegal search was conducted with the hope of discovering an informed witness to testify against Ceccolini.

> The cost of permanently silencing Hennessey is too great for an even-handed system of law enforcement to bear in order to secure such a speculative and very likely negligible deterrent effect.

United States v. New York Telephone Co., 434 U.S. 159 (1977)

Facts: With probable cause to believe that telephones at a particular premise were being used in furtherance of illegal gambling operations, a federal district court authorized FBI agents to install and use pen registers on the phones. (A pen register records numbers dialed on a telephone but does not intercept oral communications.) Invoking authority under the All Writs Act, 28 U.S. Code 1651(a), the court also ordered the New York Telephone Company to provide at prevailing rates whatever technical or other assistance was necessary to permit the agents to deploy the pen registers unobtrusively. The company's motion to vacate the order as lacking any statutory or other legal foundation was denied. The court of appeals reversed on the ground that the order constituted an abuse of discretion.

Question: Was the district court's order compelling New York Telephone to furnish assistance to FBI agents regarding the installation of pen registers authorized by the All Writs Act?

Decision: Yes. Opinion by Justice White. Vote: 5–4, Brennan, Stewart, Marshall, and Stevens dissenting in part.

Reasons: Pen registers do not intercept wire or oral communications and thus their use is not circumscribed by Title III of the Omnibus Crime Control and Safe Streets Act. Rule 41(b) of the Federal Rules of Criminal Procedure grants district courts the power to authorize the use of pen registers to obtain evidence of criminal wrongdoing. The All Writs Act authorizes federal courts to issue "all writs necessary or appropriate in aid of their respective jurisdictions." This authority "extends, under appropriate circumstances, to persons who though not parties to the original action or engaged in wrongdoing are in a position to frustrate implementation of a court order or the proper administration of justice."

Here, the company's telephone facilities were being employed to advance a criminal enterprise. Without the company's assistance, installation of the pen registers without tipping off the targets of the investigation was virtually impossible. The assistance ordered by the district court, moreover, placed no burden on the company, since it was to be compensated, and no disruption of its operations was required. In these circumstances, the district court properly concluded that enlisting the aid of the company was appropriate to prevent frustration of its warrant authorizing the installation of pen registers.

Scott v. United States, 436 U.S. 128 (1978)

Facts: A provision of the Omnibus Crime Control and Safe Streets Act of 1968, 18 U.S. Code 2518(5), requires that judicially authorized wiretapping or electronic surveillance "be conducted in such a way as to minimize the interception of communications not otherwise subject to interception under this chapter." Federal agents obtained judicial approval to wiretap a telephone that it suspected was being used in furtherance of a large conspiracy to import and distribute narcotics. Interceptions of conversations throughout a thirty-day period led to the indictment of fourteen persons. Two defendants moved to suppress the conversations on the ground that the agents monitoring the wiretap had defied the minimization requirement of section 2518(5) by intercepting all calls irrespective of whether they were related to narcotics. Granting the motion, the district court concluded that section 2518(5) had been violated because the agents failed to make an attempt in good faith to minimize interceptions that were unrelated to illicit activity. The court of appeals reversed, holding that section 2518(5) is not offended if minimization is reasonable when it is measured against the number of conversations actually intercepted, even if the monitoring agents subjectively lacked an intent to minimize.

Question: Should compliance with the minimization requirement of section 2518(5) be tested against the number of conversations actually intercepted and other objective factors rather than the subjective intent of the monitoring agents?

Decision: Yes. Opinion by Justice Rehnquist. Vote: 7–2, Brennan and Marshall dissenting.

41

Reasons: The constitutionality of searches and seizures under the Fourth Amendment is examined under a standard of objective reasonableness without regard to the underlying intent or motivation of the officers involved. Neither the language nor legislative history of the Omnibus Crime Control Act suggests an intent to depart from this objective standard in testing compliance with section 2518(5).

In applying an objective standard of reasonableness, the percentage and duration of nonpertinent calls intercepted, the scope of the illegality under investigation, the type of use to which the telephone is normally put, and the point during the authorized period of surveillance at which the interception was made are all relevant. These factors absolve the questioned wiretap in this case from any taint of failure to minimize. Although 60 percent of the intercepted calls were innocent, most were short or ambiguous and offered no opportunity for determination of their relevance to the wide-ranging conspiracy under investigation before they were completed. Some of the nonpertinent conversations were nonrecurring, moreover, and could not have been placed in a category of innocent calls, which should not have been intercepted. Although seven intercepted conversations ultimately were not material to the investigation, their brevity and ambiguity made the interceptions reasonable.

Bordenkircher v. *Hayes,* 434 U.S. 357 (1978)

Facts: Indicted for uttering a forged instrument, the accused, accompanied by retained counsel, entered into plea-bargaining negotiations with the prosecutor. Offering to recommend a five-year prison sentence in exchange for a plea of guilty, the prosecutor warned that a failure to accept would cause him to seek a more serious indictment under a habitual-offender statute, which would subject the accused to a mandatory sentence of life imprisonment by reason of his two earlier felony convictions. After declining the offer, the accused was indicted under the more punitive statute, convicted, and sentenced to a life term in the penitentiary. A federal court of appeals overturned the conviction in habeas corpus proceedings, reasoning that a prosecutor acts vindictively and in violation of due process of law by threatening a defendant during plea negotiations with more severe charges if he declines to plead guilty to the initial charge.

Question: Is the due process clause of the Fourteenth Amendment offended when a state prosecutor carries out a threat made during plea negotiations to reindict the accused on more serious charges if he declines to plead guilty to the offense with which he was originally charged?

Decision: No. Opinion by Justice Stewart. Vote: 5–4, Blackmun, Brennan, Marshall, and Powell dissenting.

Reasons: Earlier decisions in *North Carolina* v. *Pearce*, 395 U.S. 711 (1969), and *Blacklege* v. *Perry*, 417 U.S. 21 (1974), established that due process prohibits state prosecutors or judges from seeking or imposing enhanced criminal penalties as retaliation against the accused for lawfully attacking his conviction through the judicial process. This constitutional principle, however, offers no protection to an accused during plea-bargaining negotiations. A prosecutor's bargaining position is not infected with elements of "punishment or retaliation so long as the accused is free to accept or reject the prosecutor's offer." Inherent in the legitimacy of plea bargaining is the recognition that pleas of guilty are not constitutionally flawed simply because they were induced by the fear of a greater penalty upon conviction after a trial. By sanctioning plea bargaining in *Brady* v. *United States*, 397 U.S. 742 (1970), and *North Carolina* v. *Alford*, 400 U.S. 25 (1971), the Court "has necessarily accepted as constitutionally legitimate the simple reality that the prosecutor's interest at the bargaining table is to persuade the defendant to forego his right to plead not guilty." Accordingly, no constitutional taint attaches to a prosecutor's exercise of his charging discretion to induce pleas of guilty.

> There is no doubt that the breadth of discretion that our country's legal system vests in prosecuting attorneys carries with it the potential for both individual and institutional abuse. And broad though that discretion may be, there are undoubtedly constitutional limits upon its exercise. We hold only that the course of conduct engaged in by the prosecutor in this case, which no more than openly presented the defendant with the unpleasant alternatives of foregoing trial or facing charges on which he was plainly subject to prosecution, did not violate the Due Process Clause of the Fourteenth Amendment.

Criminal Law: Rights of the Accused

Criminal defendants did not depart from the 1977–1978 term empty-handed. They succeeded in knocking out five-member juries and death-penalty sentencing procedures that circumscribed the opportunity of the accused to offer mitigating evidence. In addition, the Court grudgingly expanded the exclusionary rule to cover evidence obtained by the exploitation of constitutionally flawed search warrants. Scrupulous constitutional protection was also offered to co-defendants whose representation by the same attorney created problems with respect to conflict of interest. On the other hand, defendants may be discouraged from testifying on their own behalf as a result of a decision permitting a trial judge to be influenced in deciding upon a sentence by his belief that the defendant testified falsely. And if a defendant declines to testify, the Court ruled that he may not prevent the trial judge from instructing the jury to draw no adverse inference from this fact.

In *Ballew* v. *Georgia,* 435 U.S. 223 (1978), the Court held that the use of five-person juries in criminal cases offended the Sixth Amendment right to trial by jury as applied to the states by the Fourteenth Amendment. The Court had earlier endorsed six-person juries in *Williams* v. *Florida,* 399 U.S. 78 (1970).

Doing an about-face from its controversial decision in *Furman* v. *Georgia,* 408 U.S. 238 (1972), which invalidated the nation's entire array of death-penalty statutes for inadequate restraints on the discretion of the sentencing authority, the Court, in *Lockett* v. *Ohio,* 438 U.S. 586 (1978), condemned an Ohio capital-punishment law for circumscribing the types of evidence that could be considered in mitigation by the sentencing judge. Writing for a plurality of four, Chief Justice Burger concluded that except perhaps for murder committed by a prisoner under a life sentence, the Eighth Amendment requires in capital cases that the sentencing authority consider *"as a mitigating factor,* any aspect of a defendant's character or record and any of the circumstances of the offense that the defendant proffers as a basis for a sentence less than death." *Lockett* declined to reach the question of whether the Eighth Amendment under any circumstances could tolerate capital punishment for felony murder in which the defendant played no personal role in the homicide.

Criminal defendants achieved a narrow expansion of the exclusionary rule in *Franks* v. *Delaware,* 438 U.S. 154 (1978). The Fourth Amendment, said the Court, permits a defendant to attack the constitutionality of a facially valid search warrant by establishing that its supporting affidavit contained material and intentional or reckless misrepresentations of the affiant. To justify an inquiry into the evidence concerning that issue, the Court emphasized, the defendant must allege particular deliberate falsehoods of the affiant and accompany them with an offer of proof. The Court left open the question of whether a warrant could be challenged on the ground that its supporting affidavit contained falsehoods deliberately communicated by a nongovernment informant but believed in good faith by the affiant.

The right to counsel guaranteed by the Sixth Amendment provided the foundation for victory by three codefendants in *Holloway* v. *Arkansas*, 435 U.S. 475 (1978). In that case, defense counsel representing all the codefendants moved the appointment of separate counsel because of possible conflicts of interest. Without exploring the risk of actual conflicts, the trial judge denied the motion. Holding that the denial deprived the defendants of effective assistance of counsel guaranteed by the Sixth Amendment, the Court concluded that requests for separate counsel made on the basis of alleged threatened or actual conflicts of interest must be granted absent findings that the allegations are unfounded. In addition, the Court stated, the failure to appoint separate counsel when it is constitutionally mandated requires automatic reversal of any conviction, whether or not prejudice has been proved.

Criminal defendants might be hesitant to testify in the wake of *Unites States* v. *Grayson*, 438 U.S. 41 (1978). There the Court held that neither due process nor federal statutes preclude a judge's consulting his personal belief that the defendant committed perjury or otherwise testified falsely in determining the appropriate sentence. A defendant who is inclined not to testify to avoid the repercussions at sentencing permitted by *Grayson* may be faced with a tactical dilemma in light of the ruling in *Lakeside* v. *Oregon*, 435 U.S. 333 (1978). There the Court held that neither the defendant's Fifth Amendment right against self-incrimination nor his Sixth Amendment right to counsel can prevent a trial judge from instructing the jury that no adverse inference may be drawn from his failure to testify. In *Lakeside*, the defendant opposed such an instruction because he believed that it was tantamount to waving a red flag before the jury.

Ballew v. *Georgia*, 435 U.S. 223 (1978)

Facts: Convicted of a misdemeanor by a jury of five persons and sentenced to imprisonment for one year, Ballew sought reversal of the verdict on the ground that it was obtained in violation of the right to a jury trial guaranteed by the Sixth and Fourteenth Amendments. He urged that a five-person jury in criminal cases was constitutionally inadequate to safeguard the core values of a jury trial that are protected by the amendment. A state court of appeals rejected this contention and affirmed the conviction.

Question: Does the use of five-person juries in criminal cases offend the right to jury trial guaranteed by the Sixth and Fourteenth amendments?

Decision: Yes. Plurality opinion by Justice Blackmun. Vote: 9–0, White, Powell, Burger, and Rehnquist concurring in the judgment, Brennan, Stewart, and Marshall joining the opinion in part.

Reasons: The Sixth Amendment right to a jury trial was designed to forestall government oppression by offering an accused a jury of his peers as a barrier against overzealous prosecutors and biased judges. In *Williams* v. *Florida,* 399 U.S. 78 (1970), the Court held that six-person juries could fulfill this function and thus were beyond reproach under the Sixth Amendment. Five-person juries, however, pose a critical threat to the constitutional values nurtured by jury trials. Recent empirical data suggest that juries of this size, when compared with larger juries, may thwart effective deliberation and increase the number of inaccurate verdicts, most of which will prejudice defendants. In addition, five-person juries add significantly to the likelihood that minorities or other identifiable groups will be excluded from jury service. In sum,

> the purpose and functioning of the jury in a criminal trial is seriously impaired, and to a constitutional degree, by reduction in size to below six members. . . . Because of the fundamental importance of the jury trial to the American system of criminal justice, any . . . reduction that promotes inaccurate and possibly biased decisionmaking, that causes untoward differences in verdicts, and that prevents juries from truly representing their communities, attains constitutional significance.

The minor savings in court time and costs that five-person juries offer are insufficient justification for their wholesale assault on Sixth Amendment values.

Lockett v. Ohio, 438 U.S. 586 (1978)

Facts: A jury found Lockett guilty of aggravated murder under Ohio law for knowingly participating in a robbery in which the victim was killed by a coconspirator. Lockett had driven a car to the scene of the robbery and helped the coconspirator escape and conceal incriminating evidence. Ohio law mandates the death sentence for aggravated murder unless the trial judge finds by a preponderance of the evidence that the victim had induced or facilitated the offense; the convicted offender acted under duress, coercion, or strong provocation; or the offense was primarily the offspring of psychosis or mental deficiency. Finding an absence of these mitigating factors, the trial judge sentenced Lockett to death. She attacked the sentence unsuccessfully in the Ohio Supreme Court on the ground, *inter alia*, that the Eighth Amendment compelled consideration of a broader range of mitigating circumstances than was permitted under the Ohio death penalty law.

Question: Does the Eighth Amendment require in virtually all capital cases that the sentencing authority consider as a mitigating factor any aspect of the defendant's character or record and any of the circumstances of the offense that the defendant proffers as a basis for a sentence less than death?

Decision: Yes. Plurality opinion by Chief Justice Burger. Vote: 5–3, Blackmun concurring in part and concurring in the judgment; Marshall concurring in the judgment; White concurring in part, concurring in the judgment and dissenting in part; Rehnquist concurring in part and dissenting in part.

Reasons: Woodson v. *North Carolina,* 428 U.S. 280 (1976), established the principle that the Eighth Amendment prohibition against cruel and unusual punishment invalidates virtually any death sentence imposed without consideration of the character of the offender and the circumstances of the offense. (It left open the question of whether a mandatory death sentence for murderers already serving life sentences would survive constitutional scrutiny.) Unlike other sentences, the death penalty may not be corrected or modified on the basis of postconviction behavior or information. This underscores the need for consideration of the offender as an individual before the death sentence is imposed.

[A] statute that prevents the sentencer in all capital cases from giving independent mitigating weight to aspects of the defendant's character and record and to circumstances of the offense proffered in mitigation creates the risk that the death penalty will be imposed in spite of factors which may call for a less severe penalty. When the choice is between life and death, that risk is unacceptable and incompatible with the commands of the Eighth and Fourteenth Amendments.

Franks v. *Delaware,* **438 U.S. 154 (1978)**

Facts: Relying on the Fourth Amendment, an accused moved to suppress evidence obtained in the execution of a search warrant on the ground that factual statements in an affidavit by a police officer to support the warrant were untruthful. The trial judge denied the motion, the accused was convicted, and the conviction was affirmed by the Delaware Supreme Court. It held that under no circumstances may a defendant challenge the truthfulness of a sworn statement used by police to obtain a search warrant.

Question: Does the Fourth Amendment ever offer an accused a right to challenge the veracity of factual statements made by the affiant in an affidavit supporting the issuance of a search warrant?

Decision: Yes. Opinion by Justice Blackmun. Vote: 7–2, Rehnquist and Burger dissenting.

Reasons: Warrants may be issued under the Fourth Amendment to search for evidence of crime only upon a showing of probable cause supported by oath or affirmation. Implicit in this safeguard against overzealous investigators is a requirement that the warrant affidavit contain statements that the affiant believes are true.

> Because it is the magistrate who must determine independently whether there is probable cause, it would be an unthinkable imposition upon his authority if a warrant affidavit, revealed after the fact to contain a deliberately or recklessly false statement, were to stand beyond impeachment.

To deter police misconduct while avoiding a plethora of wasteful, time-consuming hearings, the following rules are to govern challenges to the veracity of warrant affidavits:

> To mandate an evidentiary hearing, the challenger's attack must be more than conclusory and must be supported by more than a mere desire to cross-examine. There must be allegations of deliberate falsehood or of reckless disregard for the truth, and those allegations must be accompanied by an offer of proof. They should point out specifically the portion of the warrant affidavit that is claimed to be false; and they should be accompanied by a statement of supporting reasons. . . .Allegations of negligence or innocent mistake are insufficient. The deliberate falsity or reckless disregard whose impeachment is permitted today is only that of the

affiant, not of any nongovernmental informant. Finally, if these requirements are met, and if, when material that is the subject of the alleged falsity or reckless disregard is set to one side, there remains sufficient content in the warrant affidavit to support a finding of probable cause, no hearing is required. On the other hand, if the remaining content is insufficient, the defendant is entitled, under the Fourth Amendment, to his hearing.

Holloway v. *Arkansas,* 435 U.S. 475 (1978)

Facts: Three codefendants made timely motions for appointment of separate counsel on the basis of a representation by their appointed counsel that his receipt of confidential information would create a conflict of interest if the trial testimony of one tended to implicate the others. The trial judge denied the motions and the jury returned verdicts of guilty against the codefendants. On appeal, they urged that their representation by a single appointed attorney faced with conflicting loyalties violated their Sixth Amendment rights to effective assistance of counsel. Affirming the convictions, the Arkansas Supreme Court ruled that the absence of separate counsel was not reversible error, because the trial judge had not been apprised of the nature of the confidential information received by the codefendants' attorney and how it might affect his defense tactics and because none of the codefendants had implicated the others while testifying.

Question: Does the failure to appoint separate counsel upon a representation by defense counsel that possible conflicts of interest exist or to take adequate steps to determine whether that risk is remote violate the codefendants' Sixth Amendment rights to effective assistance of counsel?

Decision: Yes. Opinion by Chief Justice Burger. Vote: 6–3, Powell, Blackmun, and Rehnquist dissenting.

Reasons: In *Glasser* v. *United States,* 315 U.S. 60 (1942), the Court held that the Sixth Amendment right to counsel prohibits a court order requiring that one attorney simultaneously represent conflicting interests of criminal defendants. Once a trial judge has been notified of the possibility of a conflict, the Court reasoned, he must refrain from insisting on concurrent representation absent proof that the alleged conflict is without foundation. In this case, the trial judge refused to appoint separate counsel without exploring the merits of the alleged conflict of interest confronted by the codefendants' attorney or finding that the requests were made for dilatory purposes. This refusal offended the rationale of *Glasser* and the rights of the codefendants to effective assistance of counsel. *Glasser* mandates automatic reversal whenever a trial court improperly requires joint representation over timely objection.

United States v. *Grayson,* 438 U.S. 41 (1978)

Facts: In imposing a two-year prison sentence for escape from prison, a district court was influenced in part by its conclusion that the accused had fabricated a defense and committed perjury at trial. The court of appeals vacated the sentence, holding that a judge may not consider the defendant's veracity at trial in making the sentencing decision.

Question: In imposing a sentence after conviction, does due process preclude consideration by a trial judge of his belief that the defendant testified falsely?

Decision: No. Opinion by Chief Justice Burger. Vote: 6–3, Stewart, Brennan, and Marshall dissenting.

Reasons: A sentencing judge may legitimately consider a defendant's prospects for rehabilitation and his threat to society in imposing a sentence. The truthfulness or mendacity of a defendant under oath is clearly relevant to these concerns. When a sentencing judge, on the basis of personal observation, believes that a defendant has testified falsely and makes that fact relevant to his sentencing decision, due process is not offended simply because no formal conviction for perjury has been entered. In such circumstances, the sentencing judge is not punishing the alleged false testimony as a crime but simply using it to evaluate the defendant's prospects for rehabilitation and society's need for protection. The integrity of judges and fidelity to their oaths of office are adequate safeguards against disguised use of the sentencing process to punish alleged perjury without a formal criminal trial.

It is urged that a defendant will be unconstitutionally "chilled" in exercising his statutory and perhaps constitutional right to testify on his own behalf if the trial judge may consider his belief in the untruthfulness of the testimony in imposing sentence. This argument is unpersuasive. There is no protected right to commit perjury, and it is fanciful to suggest that an unconvicted defendant's decision to testify truthfully would be affected by the possibility that the trial judge would disbelieve the testimony and consider it negatively in imposing sentence once a verdict of guilty had been entered.

Lakeside v. Oregon, 435 U.S. 333 (1978)

Facts: A defendant declined to testify on his own behalf in a state criminal proceeding. Over his attorney's objection, the trial judge instructed the jury that no adverse inference could be drawn from the defendant's failure to testify. The instruction was necessary, the trial judge believed, to protect the defendant. The jury returned a verdict of guilty, which was sustained by the state supreme court. It rejected the argument that the instruction infringed the defendant's Fifth Amendment privilege against compulsory self-incrimination and his Sixth Amendment right to the assistance of counsel.

Question: Does either the Fifth or Sixth Amendment prohibit a trial judge from instructing a jury, over the objection of counsel, to draw no adverse inference from a defendant's failure to testify?

Decision: No. Opinion by Justice Stewart. Vote: 6–2, Stevens and Marshall dissenting. Brennan did not participate.

Reasons: In *Griffin v. California,* 380 U.S. 609 (1965), the Court held that the Fifth Amendment forbids an instruction authorizing a jury to draw an unfavorable inference from a defendant's failure to testify in a criminal case. The rationale of *Griffin* was that the questioned instruction exerted an unconstitutional compulsion to testify by exacting a penalty for the defendant's invocation of the Fifth Amendment privilege. Here, in contrast, the contested instruction was favorable to the defendant and could have exerted little if any pressure to testify. The instruction cannot be condemned simply because it may have been a red flag to the jury and underscored the defendant's failure to testify. "The very purpose of a jury charge is to flag the jurors' attention to concepts that must not be misunderstood, such as reasonable doubt and burden of proof. To instruct them in the meaning of the privilege against compulsory self-incrimination is no different."

The flaw in the defendant's Fifth Amendment argument topples his Sixth Amendment claim as well. The right to counsel does not confer a veto power over the wholly permissible actions of a trial judge. The judge has the ultimate responsibility for the conduct of a fair trial, and "[w]e cannot accept the proposition that the right to counsel, precious though it be, can operate to prevent a court from instructing a jury in the basic constitutional principles that govern the administration of criminal justice."

Freedom of Speech, Press, and Religion

The Court's 1977–1978 term witnessed a continuing First Amendment assault on professional disciplinary rules that curtail competition among attorneys in the solicitation of clients. Last term, a state law prohibiting truthful newspaper advertising of routine legal services was invalidated in *Bates* v. *State Bar of Arizona*, 433 U.S. 350 (1977). This term, the Court concluded, in *Ohralik* v. *Ohio State Bar Association*, 436 U.S. 447 (1978), that solicitation of clients in person by attorneys is a form of commercial speech entitled to the shelter of the First Amendment. Although it sustained sanctions against an attorney for soliciting clients in circumstances pregnant with opportunities for overreaching, *Ohralik* strongly suggested that solicitation would be constitutionally immune from attack if stringent safeguards against abuse or wrongdoing were embraced. In addition, the direct solicitation of clients by nonprofit public-interest groups for the purpose of litigating in furtherance of political or ideological objectives was offered virtually impregnable First Amendment protection in *In re Primus*, 436 U.S. 412 (1978). There the Court overturned a disciplinary sanction imposed on an attorney for soliciting a woman on behalf of the American Civil Liberties Union to sue her physician for allegedly exacting her consent to sterilization by threatening termination of her Medicaid benefits.

The growth of government regulation and political controls over the economy has spawned in corporations a proliferation of political action committees[2] that are lawfully empowered to contribute up to $5,000 a candidate in elections to federal office.[3] Contributions to political action committees, however, must be made voluntarily by individuals. Contributions from corporate funds are prohibited.[4] The viability of this wholesale ban on corporate involvement in political campaigns was placed in constitutional jeopardy by the ruling in *First National Bank of Boston* v. *Bellotti*, 435 U.S. 765 (1978). In that case it

---

[2] There were more than 700 active corporate political action committees during the period 1977–1978 with receipts of more than $10 million.
[3] 2 U.S. Code 441a.
[4] 2 U.S. Code 441b.

was held that, at least with regard to referenda, corporations may not be prohibited from expending corporate funds to express their views on the issues at stake.

The Court displayed steadfast resistance to attempts by broadcasters and the press to publicize government records and information about government facilities and to shield their operations from government scrutiny under the banner of the First Amendment. A unifying theme of these judicial rebuffs was that the media are on a constitutional parity with the ordinary citizen in searching for news and in resisting the authority of government investigators.

A torrent of criticism greeted the decision in *Zurcher* v. *Stanford Daily*, 436 U.S. 547 (1978), in which it was held that neither the press nor other innocent persons are constitutionally entitled to special protection against warrants to search their premises for evidence of crime. In *Zurcher* the argument was rejected that because of their chilling effect on newsgathering, search warrants against the press could be issued only after a showing that a subpoena seeking the evidence of crime would be dishonored.

The constitutional regime of parity was invoked in *Houchins* v. *KQED, Inc.*, 438 U.S. 1 (1978), to deny a broadcaster special access to a county jail for the purpose of gathering and disseminating news about prison conditions. Speaking for a plurality of three, Chief Justice Burger declared: "Neither the First Amendment nor Fourteenth Amendment mandates a right of access to government information or sources of information within the government's control."

A First Amendment quest by the media to copy for broadcasting and sale to the public the tapes of President Nixon that were introduced in the Watergate cover-up trial was repudiated in *Nixon* v. *Warner Communications, Inc.*, 435 U.S. 589 (1978). Since members of the public were not granted physical access to the tapes for copying, the Court explained, members of the media lacked any constitutional right to such access.

The First Amendment also proved impotent to shelter the media from regulatory oversight by the Federal Communications Commission (FCC) in a pair of decisions. In *FCC* v. *National Citizens Committee for Broadcasting*, 436 U.S. 775 (1978), the Court upheld a rule that prospectively barred the formation of commonly owned newspapers and broadcasting stations that would serve identical markets. Noting the benefit to the public from exposure to a diversity of voices among the media and the ideological neutrality of the rule, the Court found no constitutional infirmity in prohibiting newspapers from obtaining broadcast licenses in markets where their views are already heard.

A sharply divided Court in *FCC* v. *Pacifica Foundation*, 438 U.S.

726 (1978), voted to uphold the commission's rebuke of a radio station for its daytime broadcasting of indecent words voiced by satirist George Carlin. Writing for a 5-4 majority, Justice Stevens explained that the narrow First Amendment question was whether indecent speech that could be disseminated through nonbroadcast outlets could be excluded from the airwaves at times when youthful listeners were likely to be among the audience. Answering in the affirmative, Stevens found sufficient justification for the suppression of such broadcasts in their threats to parental control over childrearing and to the privacy of the home.

The sole First Amendment triumph for the press emerged, somewhat ironically, from investigative reporting on allegations of judicial misconduct. The state of Virginia prosecuted a newspaper for accurately reporting the identity of a judge under investigation by a judicial review commission. Under state law, the identity of the judge was confidential information, and its disclosure before the filing of any formal complaint was a crime. In *Landmark Communications, Inc.* v. *Virginia*, 435 U.S. 829 (1978), the Court invalidated the conviction of the newspaper. The strong interest of the First Amendment in subjecting government officials and affairs to the scrutiny of the press, the Court explained, superseded any interest of the state in confidentiality, unless breach of confidentiality would threaten the fair administration of justice. Since the state failed to prove that publicly identifying the judge under investigation created such a threat, the Court stated, the conviction ran afoul of the First Amendment.

The First and Fourteenth amendments generally proscribe government sponsorship of religion through financial aid or otherwise. This proscription condemns government programs offering financial support to religiously affiliated schools unless three tests are satisfied: the program must have a secular purpose, its principal or primary effect must neither advance nor inhibit religion, and it must avoid fostering excessive entanglement between government and religion. In *Levitt* v. *Committee for Public Education*, 413 U.S. 472 (1973), a New York statute that reimbursed private schools for costs incurred in performing various state-mandated testing and record-keeping services was invalidated. Its constitutional vice, said the Court, was its advancement of religion. In *New York* v. *Cathedral Academy*, 434 U.S. 125 (1977), the Court blocked an attempt to circumvent the decision in *Committee for Public Education* by condemning New York's reimbursement of private schools for testing and record-keeping expenditures that antedated that earlier ruling.

In *McDaniel* v. *Paty*, 435 U.S. 618 (1978), a Tennessee minister invoked the free exercise clause of the First Amendment to sweep away a statutory barrier to his candidacy for public office. To forestall political divisiveness and rancor along religious lines, Tennessee disqualified ministers from serving as legislators or delegates to a constitutional convention. Holding that that disqualification imposed an unconstitutional burden on the free exercise of religion, the Court observed that history had discredited fears that participation by the clergy in the political process would engender religious strife or state entanglement in religious affairs.

Ohralik v. *Ohio State Bar Association*, 436 U.S. 447 (1978)

Facts: Informed that a casual acquaintance (McClintock) and her eighteen-year-old passenger (Holbert) had been hospitalized because of an automobile accident, an Ohio attorney visited the two for the purpose of offering his legal services to recover damages. The attorney obtained McClintock's consent to a contingency fee arrangement after he had made an unsolicited visit to her hospital room and after a secret tape recording had been made of a conversation between the attorney and her parents about rights under an insurance policy. Holbert also agreed to a contingency fee contract after the attorney had visited her at home, at which time he explained her rights under the insurance policy. The attorney recorded most of this conversation by means of a concealed tape recorder. Subsequently, both McClintock and Holbert discharged the attorney and filed complaints against him with a county bar association. The association filed a formal complaint with a state disciplinary board, which found that the attorney had violated the Ohio Code of Professional Responsibility in soliciting business from McClintock and Holbert. Suspending the attorney for an indefinite period, the Supreme Court of Ohio rejected the argument that his questioned conduct was a form of commercial speech shielded from challenge under the First Amendment.

Question: Does the First Amendment prohibit the imposition of sanctions against an attorney who solicits clients in person for pecuniary gain?

Decision: No. Opinion by Justice Powell. Vote: 8–0, Marshall concurring in part and concurring in the judgment, Rehnquist concurring in the judgment. Brennan did not participate.

Reasons: The First Amendment tolerates greater government regulation of commercial speech than of noncommercial speech because the former makes a lesser contribution to the political intercourse that the amendment was intended to cultivate. Commercial speech, nevertheless, may not be suppressed in the absence of important countervailing government interests.

In this case, the commercial speech that triggered the disciplinary sanctions consisted of the attorney's solicitation of McClintock and Holbert in person to convey information about his availability and his fees. Nothing in the Code of Professional Responsibility tainted his communications about the legal rights and remedies of the two so long as the information was not used as bait to obtain an agreement to represent them for a fee. The attorney was punished only because he combined commercial speech with an effort to exact contingency fee arrangements. Unlike the newspaper advertising of routine legal services that received constitutional endorsement in *Bates* v. *State Bar of Arizona*, 433 U.S. 350 (1977), solicitation in person of the type condemned here threatens to obstruct free and informed decisionmaking by prospective clients.

> [I]n-person solicitation may exert pressure and often demands an immediate response, without providing an opportunity for comparison or reflection. The aim and effect of in-person solicitation may be to provide a one-sided presentation and to encourage speedy and perhaps uninformed decisionmaking; there is no opportunity for intervention or counter-education by agencies of the Bar, supervisory authorities, or persons close to the solicited individual. . . . In-person solicitation is as likely as not to discourage persons needing counsel from engaging in a critical comparison of the "availability, nature, and prices" of legal services.

Prohibitions against solicitation also seek to forestall overreaching by attorneys, invasions of individual privacy, and legal advice that is distorted by an attorney's pecuniary self-interest. These are all important government interests that justify suppression of the commercial speech element of solicitation in person. The First Amendment may not be invoked to shield an attorney from sanctions for violating antisolicitation rules simply because actual proven harm to the solicited individual is lacking. The interests of the government in adopting prophylactic measures and avoiding the myriad problems of proving what transpired between an attorney and a lay person outweigh the value of any commercial speech that would be protected by mandating proof of actual harm.

In the light of these principles, there is no foundation for offering First Amendment protection to the attorney's solicitation of Mc-

Clintock and Holbert in person. He approached the two young women in circumstances in which they were vulnerable to overreaching, employed a concealed tape recorder to obtain evidence of any consent to representation, failed to explain the meaning of a contingency-fee arrangement, and resisted their requests that he cease representing them. These actions threatened the evils that the Ohio antisolicitation rules were designed to forestall and therefore stripped the attorney's commercial speech of protection under the First Amendment.

In re Primus, 436 U.S. 412 (1978)

Facts: The South Carolina Supreme Court publicly reprimanded an attorney for violating a professional disciplinary rule that condemns solicitation of clients by lawyers on behalf of nonprofit organizations that are primarily engaged in offering legal services if an associate of the lawyer is counsel for the organization. The tainted conduct stemmed from the attorney's uncompensated work on behalf of the American Civil Liberties Union (ACLU). Concerned that indigent pregnant mothers were being unlawfully sterilized or threatened with sterilization as a condition of receipt of Medicaid benefits, the attorney addressed a meeting of women who had been victimized, advised them of their legal rights, and suggested the possibility of a lawsuit. Subsequently, the ACLU notified the attorney of its willingness to represent the sterilized mothers in a lawsuit. The attorney transmitted this information to one of the mothers in a letter in which she offered to explain what a lawsuit would entail. After receiving the letter, the mother communicated her intention not to sue, and her relations with the attorney ceased. The foundation for the public reprimand consisted of the attorney's letter on behalf of the ACLU to the sterilized mother and her association with lawyers who were affiliated with the organization. The attorney's contention that the solicitation constituted a form of free expression and political association protected by the First Amendment was rejected by the South Carolina Supreme Court.

Question: Does the First Amendment prohibit a state from punishing an attorney who, seeking to advance political and ideological goals through associational activity, including litigation, advises a lay person of her legal rights and discloses in a subsequent letter that free legal assistance is available from a nonprofit organization with which the lawyer and her associates are affiliated?

Decision: Yes. Opinion by Justice Powell. Vote: 7–1, Marshall concurring in part and concurring in the judgment, Rehnquist dissenting. Brennan did not participate.

Reasons: Unlike the solicitation in person condemned in *Ohralik v. Ohio State Bar Association,* the contested conduct in this case was undertaken not for pecuniary gain but to express personal political beliefs and to advance the civil liberties objectives of the ACLU. Accordingly, the conduct was entitled to enhanced First Amendment protection under the principles embraced in *NAACP v. Button,* 371 U.S. 415 (1963). There the Court held that the NAACP and its staff attorneys enjoyed a constitutional right to solicit prospective litigants in desegregation suits for the purpose of furthering the civil-rights objectives of the organization and its members. The Court reasoned that such solicitation was a form of expressive and associational freedom at the core of the First Amendment's protective ambit and could be circumscribed only when it was clearly necessary in order to advance a strong government interest. The ACLU, like the NAACP, engages in extensive educational, lobbying, and litigating activities to advance the political values it espouses. The litigation it conducts, without remuneration from clients, is a form of political expression and association. Neither the reprimanded attorney nor her associates nor the ACLU would have received any compensation from the sterilized mother who was urged to file a lawsuit. The letter soliciting such action was thus constitutionally protected absent proof that it threatened significant substantive evils that the state has a right to prohibit.

The disciplinary action taken against the attorney was alleged to have been aimed at preventing undue influence, overreaching, misrepresentation, invasion of privacy, conflict of interest, and lay interference with the attorney-client relationship. But the record is barren of support for these allegations. The questioned letter imparted accurate factual information that was material to the making of an informed decision about whether to authorize a lawsuit by the ACLU. It involved no appreciable invasion of privacy and offered little opportunity for overreaching or coercion. Because the solicitation was in writing, it was easily policed, and there was no proof of a serious danger that the ACLU would improperly intrude on the attorney-client relationship. In these circumstances, the First Amendment principles of *Button* protected the attorney's solicitation from rebuke by the state.

A state may, of course, embrace reasonable restrictions with respect to the time, place, and manner of solicitation by members of its bar. And

> nothing in this opinion should be read to foreclose carefully tailored regulation that does not abridge unnecessarily the associational freedom of nonprofit organizations, or their members, having characteristics like those of the NAACP or the ACLU.

First National Bank of Boston v. *Bellotti,* 435 U.S. 765 (1978)

Facts: A Massachusetts criminal statute prohibits contributions or expenditures by corporations "for the purpose of . . . influencing or affecting the vote of any question submitted to the voters, other than one materially affecting any of the property, business or assets of the corporation." In addition, the statute specifically bars corporate contributions or expenditures for the purpose of influencing the vote on proposals subject to referendum that concern only the taxation of individuals. Desiring to publicize their views on a referendum that would authorize the state legislature to impose a graduated individual income tax, several corporations brought suit in which they sought a declaratory judgment condemning the statute under the First Amendment. The Supreme Judicial Court of Massachusetts rejected the attack, holding "that only when a general political issue materially affects a corporation's business, property or assets may that corporation claim First Amendment protection for its speech or other activities entitling it to communicate its position on that issue to the general public."

Question: Does the challenged statute as applied to foreclose corporate discussion of certain referendum issues offend the protection of free speech guaranteed by the First Amendment?

Decision: Yes. Opinion by Justice Powell. Vote: 5–4, White, Brennan, Marshall, and Rehnquist dissenting.

Reasons: A central purpose of the First Amendment is to protect and cultivate public discussion and informed decisionmaking with regard to government affairs. The contested statute frustrates this purpose by denying corporations the right to inform prospective voters in a referendum of their views on the wisdom of a graduated personal income tax. This "type of speech [is] indispensable to decisionmaking in a democracy, and this is no less true because the speech comes from a corporation rather than an individual." Speech does not forfeit protection under the First Amendment simply because it has a corporate rather than an individual origin. Accordingly, the prohibition against corporate speech on matters that relate to public affairs can survive constitutional scrutiny only if the state establishes that the suppression is necessary to advance a compelling government interest.

Two such interests have been proffered: encouraging citizens to participate in the electoral process, thereby forestalling diminished confidence in government, and safeguarding the rights of shareholders whose views differ from those voiced by corporate managements. The first interest is jeopardized, it is argued, if corporations monopolize discussion of an issue up for referendum and submerge individual voices. If this assertion had been substantiated by the record, it might have justified the ban on corporate speech. "But there has been no showing that the relative voice of corporations has been overwhelming or even significant in influencing referenda in Massachusetts, or that there has been any threat to the confidence of the citizenry in government." The second interest—protecting shareholders from subsidizing corporate speech with which they disagree—may be worthy of government protection. The contested statute, however, does little to advance this purpose. It does not curtail corporate activity with respect to the passage or defeat of legislation or prohibit corporate speech on issues before they are placed on a referendum ballot. It denies its protective ambit, moreover, to dissident members of business trusts, real estate investment trusts, labor unions, and other associations that may express views on electoral questions. The statute is also overbroad because it condemns corporate speech that is unanimously supported by shareholders. In addition, the fact that it singles out the graduated personal income tax for special treatment betrays an illegitimate legislative intent to suppress speech on a particular subject irrespective of the concerns of shareholders. Accordingly, even assuming that protection of shareholders is a compelling interest, it offers no justification for suppressing corporate speech in this case because the suppression lacks any substantial correlation to the safeguarding of the rights of shareholders.

Zurcher v. *Stanford Daily*, 436 U.S. 547 (1978)

Facts: Several police officers were attacked and injured during a demonstration held at the Stanford University Hospital. Two days later, the *Stanford Daily*, a student newspaper, carried articles and photographs devoted to the demonstration, suggesting that a staff member had had an opportunity to photograph the assault. Relying on these facts, a district attorney obtained a warrant authorizing an immediate search of the *Daily*'s offices for negatives, film, and pictures relevant to the identification of the assailants of the police who were alleged to have committed felonies. The affidavit for the warrant did not allege that members of the *Daily* staff were criminally involved. The search revealed no new evidence of crime.

Alleging that the search violated the First, Fourth, and Fourteenth Amendments, the *Daily* brought suit in federal district court challenging the constitutionality of warrants authorizing searches of its offices for evidence of crime. Granting declaratory relief, the district court held that the issuance of a warrant to search for materials in the possession of persons unsuspected of crime offended the Fourth and Fourteenth Amendments unless a *subpoena duces tecum* would be impracticable. Additionally, it held that when an innocent newspaper is the object of the search, the First Amendment condemns any warrant except when there is a clear showing that a subpoena would beget the destruction or removal of important evidence and a restraining order prohibiting such action would be dishonored. The court of appeals affirmed.

Question: Does either the First or Fourth Amendment condemn the issuance of warrants to search for evidence of crime in the possession of newspapers or others unsuspected of wrongdoing absent a showing that a *subpoena duces tecum* would be disobeyed?

Decision: No. Opinion by Justice White. Vote: 5–3, Stewart, Marshall, and Stevens dissenting. Brennan did not participate.

Reasons: Neither the language of the Fourth Amendment, its history, nor prior decisions expounding its purposes offer any foundation for erecting a special shield against the issuance of warrants to search for evidence of crime in the possession of innocent persons. When the government has probable cause to believe that evidence of crime may be discovered at a particular place, the invasion of privacy engendered by a search is justified irrespective of the culpability of the owner or occupant of the premises. Accordingly, courts may not invoke the overarching Fourth Amendment requirement that all searches be "reasonable" to preclude the issuance of warrants "to search for evidence simply because the owner or possessor of the place to be searched is not then reasonably suspected of criminal involvement." This holding is in part justified because insisting on subpoenas in lieu of search warrants would curtail and possibly obstruct many criminal investigations and because prosecutors will ordinarily use subpoenas when these fears are groundless, since they may issue them without judicial approval.

The First Amendment guarantee of a free press does not offer innocent newspapers special protection against search warrants. It does, however, require that scrupulous exactitude be used in describing the places and objects of any search to forestall any general rummaging through books, papers, newspaper files, and other materials protected by the First Amendment. The preconditions for a warrant to search a newspaper office—probable cause, specificity with respect to the place to be searched and the things to be seized, and overall reasonableness—are adequate safeguards against any disruption, harassment, or self-censorship of the press that warrants may threaten .

The lack of an opportunity by the press to litigate the propriety of a search warrant before the seizure of First Amendment materials in its possession, it is urged, imposes a prior restraint on free expression. A neutral magistrate, however, has both the power and duty to prevent the use of search warrants as vehicles for suppressing expression that is arguably within the ambit of the First Amendment prior to a judicial determination of its legality.

> [T]he Fourth Amendment does not prevent or advise against legislative or executive efforts to establish nonconstitutional protections against possible abuses of the search warrant procedure, but we decline to reinterpret the Amendment to impose a general constitutional barrier against warrants to search newspaper premises, to require resort to subpoenas as a general rule, or to demand prior notice and hearing in connection with the issuance of search warrants.

Houchins v. KQED, Inc., 438 U.S. 1 (1978)

Facts: Prompted by the filing of a lawsuit, a county sheriff adopted a policy of limited public access to a county jail. It provided for monthly public tours in groups of twenty-five through a large portion of the facilities. The tours did not include, however, disciplinary cells or the portions of the jail where crime and adverse physical conditions were alleged to be pervasive. No cameras, tape recorders, or interviews with inmates, moreover, were permitted. A local broadcasting station brought suit in federal district court, contending that the First Amendment offered it broader access to the county jail than was available through the public tours. Granting preliminary injunctive relief, the district court enjoined the sheriff from denying news personnel of the station access to the entire jail at reasonable times and hours, with the aid of photographic and sound equipment and interviews with inmates, to provide full and accurate coverage of the institution. The court of appeals affirmed.

Question: Does the First Amendment protection of a free press confer on the news media a broader right of access to a county jail than is enjoyed by the public generally?

Decision: No. Plurality opinion by Chief Justice Burger. Vote: 4–3, Stewart concurring in the judgment, Brennan, Powell, and Stevens dissenting. Marshall and Blackmun did not participate.

Reasons: In *Pell* v. *Procunier*, 417 U.S. 817 (1974), and *Saxbe* v. *Washington Post*, 417 U.S. 843 (1974), the Court embraced the general principle that newsmen have no constitutional right of access to prisons or their inmates beyond that afforded the general public. It cannot be gainsaid that informed public debate about conditions in jails is important and that broad access of the media to jails may enhance the quality of the debate. Even without direct access, however, the news media can learn about prison conditions through letters from inmates, interviews with attorneys, visitors, or former inmates, and examinations of public reports on prisons frequently mandated by law. Whether the government should go further and open penal institutions to news broadcasters for filming and interviews with inmates is a question of policy for the political branches. "Neither the First nor Fourteenth Amendment mandates a right of access to government information or sources of information within the government's control."

Nixon v. Warner Communications, Inc., 435 U.S. 589 (1978)

Facts: During the so-called Watergate cover-up trial, twenty-two hours of taped conversations involving President Nixon were played for the jury and the public in the courtroom. The reels of tape containing the conversations were entered into evidence. Several broadcasters filed a motion with the district court seeking permission to copy, broadcast, and sell to the public the portions of the tapes played at trial. The former President opposed the application. The district court denied the motion without prejudice because it believed that widespread mass merchandising of the tapes might influence the pending appeals of four men convicted at trial. Since the press had published transcripts of the tapes, the district court explained, the public's right to know offered no justification for threatening the defendants' rights on appeal. The court of appeals reversed, holding that the common-law privilege to inspect and copy judicial records outweighed the speculative prejudice to defendants in the event a retrial was necessary. It remanded the case for development of a plan to release the tapes.

Question: Did the court of appeals err in holding that the common-law right of access to judicial records required release of the presidential tapes?

Decision: Yes. Opinion by Justice Powell. Vote: 7–2, White and Brennan dissenting in part, Marshall and Stevens dissenting.

Reasons: American courts generally recognize a common-law right to inspect and copy public records and documents, including access to judicial records and documents. This right, however, is qualified, and access to judicial records has been denied when it has been sought for "improper purposes" such as gratification of private spite, promotion of public scandal, or unfair business practices.

In this case, President Nixon has advanced several reasons for curtailing the common-law right of broadcasters to duplicate and market the presidential tapes at issue: an alleged proprietary right over commercial exploitation of his voice, invasion of privacy, presidential confidentiality, and improper commercialization of court records. Against the interests that underlie these claims must be weighed the presumption in favor of public access to judicial records and the public education that release of aural copies of the tapes would yield. In addition, the Presidential Recordings and Materials Preservation Act must be considered. That act created an administrative procedure for processing and releasing to the public, pursuant to statutory guidelines, all Nixon's materials that are of historical interest, including the tapes at issue here.

> Because of this congressionally prescribed avenue of public access we need not weigh the parties' competing arguments as though the District Court were the only potential source of information regarding these historical materials. The presence of an alternative means of public access tips the scales in favor of denying release.

Neither the First Amendment protection of a free press nor the Sixth Amendment guarantee of a public trial justifies disturbing this conclusion. The former protection generally grants the press access to court information equal but not superior to that available to the general public. Since the public was not afforded physical access to the tapes in question for copying or other purposes, the First Amendment does not shield the press from an identical restriction. The constitutional guarantee of a public trial is satisfied by the "opportunity of members of the public and the press to attend the trial and to report what they have observed." It imposes no obligation to broadcast trials live or on tape to the public. The decision whether to permit access to the tapes is best left to the sound discretion of the trial court.

Federal Communications Commission v. *National Citizens Committee for Broadcasting,* 436 U.S. 775 (1978)

Facts: Seeking to broaden the diversification of ownership of the mass media, the Federal Communications Commission issued regulations that prospectively bar the formation or transfer of a commonly owned radio or television broadcasting station and a daily newspaper located in the same community. Existing commonly located newspaper-broadcast combinations are not disturbed, except in communities in which they have no newspaper or broadcasting competitors. In these monopoly markets, divestiture of either the newspaper or the broadcasting station is required within five years, absent a justification for waiver.

Various parties assailed the regulations in the court of appeals. Broadcasters and newspaper owners urged that the commission lacked statutory authority to promulgate the regulations and that they offended the First Amendment. A group of private citizens and the Justice Department contended that the decision to sanctify most existing newspaper-broadcast combinations was arbitrary and capricious and thus ran afoul of the Administrative Procedure Act. The court of appeals affirmed the commission's prospective rules but invalidated the limited divestiture requirement.

Question: Were the commission's rules concerning common ownership of newspapers and broadcasting stations beyond statutory or constitutional reproach in all respects?

Decision: Yes. Opinion by Justice Marshall. Vote: 8–0. Brennan did not participate.

Reasons: Section 303(r) of the Communications Act empowers the commission to promulgate reasonable regulations governing the issuance of broadcast licenses "in the public interest." The contested regulations were largely the offspring of a long-standing policy of the commission to promote diversification of control of the mass communications media. The commission's prospective ban on commonly located newspaper-broadcasting combinations advances First Amendment and antitrust values and is thus consistent with its statutory mandate to regulate in the public interest.

The prospective rules are likewise invulnerable under the First Amendment. In *Red Lion Broadcasting Co.* v. *FCC,* 395 U.S. 367 (1969), the Court concluded that the First Amendment offers no redress to persons denied broadcast licenses in order to vindicate the public interest. It is urged, nevertheless, that the regulations are infirm because they are directed entirely toward newspapers and make forfeiture of the right to publish a newspaper a condition of receipt of a broadcast license. The former contention is factually inaccurate because the commission has barred all owners of the larger media of mass communications from obtaining commonly located broadcasting stations. The latter is unpersuasive because the owner of a newspaper may acquire or seek broadcast licenses in all communities where his papers do not circulate. The regulations were embraced to promote the interests of free speech, moreover, and reflect neither hostility nor sympathy toward any particular political, economic, or social views espoused by newspapers. They therefore pass First Amendment scrutiny.

Finally, the commission's decision to limit divestiture to newspaper-broadcasting combinations with an effective monopoly was rationally founded. It concluded that a more sweeping divestiture requirement might reduce local ownership of broadcasting stations, threaten the quality and continuity of programming, and unfairly deny newspaper owners who had offered meritorious broadcast service the opportunity to continue in operation. The commission's conclusion that these predictive harms to the public interest outweighed the potential benefits that increased diversification of ownership would yield was not irrational.

Federal Communications Commission v. Pacifica Foundation, 438 U.S. 726 (1978)

Facts: A radio broadcaster was rebuked by the Federal Communications Commission for its broadcast of a twelve-minute monologue entitled "Filthy Words" at two o'clock in the afternoon. Finding that the monologue was riddled with "indecent" language in violation of 18 U.S. Code 1464 and was deliberately programmed at a time when children were likely to be listening, the commission disclaimed any intent to condemn the broadcast of vulgar or offensive language aimed primarily at adult audiences. The commission's order was reversed in the court of appeals on the grounds that it constituted censorship in violation of 47 U.S. Code 326 and that no violation of section 1464 had occurred. The court did not reach the broadcaster's contention that any government sanction for broadcasting indecent but not obscene language would offend the First Amendment.

Question: Was the commission's order statutorily authorized and faithful to the First Amendment protection of free speech?

Decision: Yes. Opinion by Justice Stevens. Vote: 5–4, Powell and Blackmun concurring in part and concurring in the judgment, Brennan, Marshall, Stewart, and White dissenting.

Reasons: The commission's order is initially attacked as forbidden censorship under section 326. That section, however, only denies the commission power to edit proposed broadcasts in advance; it does not disable the commission from considering the content of past programs when considering license-renewal applications or alleged violations of section 1464.

The broadcasting of indecent language that could not constitutionally be condemned as obscene is proscribed by section 1464. The "Filthy Words" monologue ran afoul of this statutory prohibition, which was the mainspring of the commission's questioned order.

The First Amendment did not shield the monologue from the mild rebuke imposed by the commission. Indecent language is entitled to some First Amendment protection, and restrictions on broadcasting it that are inspired by hostility toward the ideas it conveys could not be countenanced. Here, however, the commission disapproved of the "Filthy Words" monologue only because of the timing of the broadcast and the type of words used to convey ideas; it was not hostile to the ideas themselves, which could have been expressed in unoffending language.

Although the monologue was not obscene and thus would be sheltered from sanctions if disseminated by the press, it was stripped of First Amendment protection when aired by radio for two reasons. The broadcast medium is uniquely pervasive and invades the privacy of the home. The audience cannot be completely protected against shocking or indecent material by prior warnings because it is continually tuning in and out. "To say that one may avoid further offense by turning off the radio when he hears indecent language is like saying that the remedy for an assault is to run away after the first blow."

In addition, broadcasting is uniquely accessible to children, even those unable to read. To protect the parent's right to rear his children without indecent language in the home and to advance the legitimate interest of the government in cultivating the well-being of its youth, the government may circumscribe indecent broadcasting that is aimed at a substantial youthful audience.

Landmark Communications v. Virginia, 435 U.S. 829 (1978)

Facts: A Virginia statute makes it a crime to divulge confidential information submitted to a state judicial review commission during an investigation of charges of judicial disability or misconduct. A newspaper was convicted under the statute for publishing an article in which a judge who was under investigation was accurately identified. On appeal, the Virginia Supreme Court rejected the contention that the conviction offended the protection of free speech and press guaranteed by the First and Fourteenth amendments.

Question: Does the First Amendment shelter persons from criminal sanctions for disclosing accurate confidential information concerning an official investigation into judicial disability or misconduct if they are strangers to the inquiry?

Decision: Yes. Opinion by Chief Justice Burger. Vote: 7–0, Stewart concurring in the judgment. Brennan and Powell did not participate.

Reasons: A central purpose of the First Amendment is the promotion and protection of public discussion and scrutiny of government affairs. The questioned publication served this purpose by disclosing accurate factual information about a legislatively authorized inquiry pending before a judicial commission. Accordingly, only a powerful countervailing state interest could justify criminally punishing the publication.

The state has an interest in maintaining the confidentiality of commission investigations until a formal charge has been filed. The filing of complaints and the cooperation of witnesses are thereby encouraged. Confidentiality also forestalls the publication of unexamined and unwarranted complaints lodged against judges. And judges may voluntarily resign or retire if the publicity that would accompany a formal charge can be avoided. Confidentiality, however, can ordinarily be secured without the use of criminal sanctions against nonparticipants in the investigatory proceedings. More than forty states have commissions that investigate charges of judicial misconduct without this weapon. Even assuming that criminal sanctions enhance the guarantee of confidentiality, moreover, fundamental First Amendment principles prohibit suppression of free speech by a state simply to protect the good repute of judges or the judicial system.

It is urged that the punished speech created a clear and present threat of injury to the judge under investigation, to the operation of the judicial commission, and to the impartial administration of justice. Thus, it is argued, the punishment was not an affront to First Amendment guarantees. The doctrine of clear and present danger, however, can be invoked only if there is solid evidence that the punished speech immediately imperils serious substantive evils. In this case, the state failed to demonstrate that the publication in question posed an imminent danger to the fair administration of justice or otherwise threatened to inflict extremely serious harm. The state may use internal procedures to safeguard the confidentiality of commission investigations, moreover, thereby largely eliminating the risk of premature disclosure. Any risks that remain must be borne by the state to avoid stifling the public scrutiny of government that the First Amendment was designed to cultivate.

New York v. *Cathedral Academy,* 434 U.S. 125 (1977)

Facts: In *Levitt* v. *Committee for Public Education,* 413 U.S. 472 (1973), the Court invalidated a New York statute authorizing reimbursement of private schools for the costs of certain record-keeping and testing services required by state law. The *Levitt* decision was founded on the view that any reimbursement would create an impermissible risk of aiding the sectarian activities of private schools in contravention of the establishment clause of the First Amendment. Thereafter, New York enacted a law entitling nonpublic schools to obtain reimbursement for expenses incurred in reliance on the statute that *Levitt* condemned. A state court of appeals ruled that the new law did not offend the establishment clause.

Question: Does the establishment clause prohibit New York from paying nonpublic schools for expenses incurred in reliance on the statute invalidated in *Levitt?*

Decision: Yes. Opinion by Justice Stewart. Vote: 6–3, Burger, Rehnquist, and White dissenting.

Reasons: The law in question authorizes state payments for the activities identical to those found in *Levitt* to contribute to religious indoctrination. The payments create the identical threat to promotion of sectarian activities that *Levitt* found offensive to the establishment clause. This constitutional infirmity cannot be remedied by seeking to restrict the payments to teacher-prepared tests and other classroom activities that advanced only secular goals. To enforce such a mandate would require detailed state scrutiny of classroom materials and behavior to filter the religious from the nonreligious. That would entail excessive government entanglement with religion, which is also condemned by the establishment clause.

There are no equitable considerations that might justify a degree of constitutional taint in state payments for sectarian services. Prior to the statute invalidated by *Levitt*, nonpublic schools were required to pay for state-mandated testing and record-keeping services. Any detrimental reliance on the condemned statute consisted of expenditures for sectarian activities that nonpublic schools might not have been able to afford without the state subsidy. This reliance interest can claim no positive weight when balanced against a "measurable constitutional violation."

McDaniel v. Paty, 435 U.S. 618 (1978)

Facts: A Tennessee statute barred ministers or priests of any denomination from serving as delegates to the state's 1977 constitutional convention. The statute was unsuccessfully attacked in state courts as an unconstitutional infringement of the free exercise of religion protected by the First Amendment. The Tennessee Supreme Court reasoned that the disqualification of clergy from elective public office did not burden religious belief as such but merely restricted religious action in the lawmaking process. This restriction was held to be justified by the strong interest of the state in preventing the establishment of religion and in forestalling divisiveness and political cleavages along religious lines.

Question: Does the free exercise clause of the First Amendment prohibit states from disqualifying the clergy from holding elective public office?

Decision: Yes. Plurality opinion by Chief Justice Burger. Vote: 8–0, Brennan, Marshall, Stewart, and White concurring in the judgment. Blackmun did not participate.

Reasons: The right to the free exercise of religion encompasses the right to preach, proselyte, and perform similar ministerial functions. The questioned clergy-disqualification statute requires the surrender of this right as a condition of holding elective office. This burden on the exercise of constitutionally protected religious conduct can be justified only if it is necessary in order to advance a state interest of the highest order. Tennessee urges that its contested statute is necessary to ensure fidelity to the establishment clause of the First Amendment because ministers in public office will exercise their authority to promote the interests of one sect, thwart the interests of others, and encourage political confrontations along religious lines.

> However widely that view may have been held in the 18th century by many, including enlightened statesmen of that day, the American experience provides no persuasive support for the fear that clergymen in public office will be less careful of antiestablishment interests or less faithful to their oaths of civil office than their unordained counterparts.

Accordingly, the clergy-disqualification statute fails to advance a sufficiently strong interest of the state to save it from condemnation under the free exercise clause.

Civil Rights and Civil Liberties

The Court's pioneering exploration of the constitutionality of affirmative action programs in *Regents of the University of California* v. *Bakke,* 438 U.S. 265 (1978), produced a decision symbolic of its mixed approach to claims of civil rights and civil liberties during the 1977–1978 term. Dividing the Court into three fairly distinct blocs, the *Bakke* ruling invalidated a strict racial quota used in a program of admissions to a state medical school, but endorsed less rigid forms of affirmative action in which preference is shown for minority groups solely on account of race. This type of cautious and moderate jurisprudence also marked the Court's encounters with claims concerning constitutional torts, procedural due process, and discrimination in employment.

Liability for Constitutional Torts. In seven decisions, the Court explored the scope of federal, state, and municipal liability for constitutional torts. They expanded the liability of federal executive officials, states, and municipalities, denied any recourse to those injured by judicial or quasi-judicial officers, and expounded the type of relief available to victims of constitutional wrongdoing. In *Butz* v. *Economou*, 438 U.S. 478 (1978), a dealer in commodities futures sued the secretary of agriculture, the assistant secretary, administrative judicial officers, and government attorneys, alleging that they had committed constitutional violations in connection with their participation in the adjudication of an administrative complaint charging the dealer with regulatory infractions. The defendants moved to dismiss the complaint, on the theory that federal executive officers are absolutely immune to liability for damage in connection with acts committed within the scope of their official duties. Disavowing the implications of *Spalding* v. *Vilas*, 161 U.S. 483 (1896), and *Barr* v. *Matteo*, 360 U.S. 564 (1959), in which it was held that federal officials were invulnerable to damage suits for common-law torts, the Court refused to grant an identical shield for constitutional violations. To extend absolute immunity to all federal executive officials, the Court said, would erode constitutional protections and incentives to adhere to constitutional norms. A qualified immunity that shields executive officers from liability for damages in connection with constitutional torts only if they believed, in good faith, in the propriety of their conduct, the Court concluded, will generally accommodate the need for vigorous executive action while forestalling constitutional abuses. Thus, the Court stated, federal executive officials may be held accountable in damages for conduct that they knew or should have known exceeded clearly established constitutional limits.[5] The *Economou* Court explained, however, that the public interest in fearless advocacy and decisionmaking in the adjudication of criminal or administrative complaints justified clothing with absolute immunity the actions taken by key participants in furtherance of prosecutorial or judicial functions. Accordingly, it held that administrative judicial officers in resolving complaints, officials in initiating administrative proceedings, and attorneys in prosecuting administrative complaints are not answerable for damages even if they intentionally violated the plaintiff's constitutional rights.

Victims of unconstitutional action garnered important victories in *Monell* v. *Department of Social Services of the City of New York*, 436

---

[5] Under 42 U.S. Code 1983, state executive officials enjoy the identical qualified immunity with respect to constitutional torts. Scheuer v. Rhodes, 416 U.S. 232 (1974).

U.S. 658 (1978), and *Hutto* v. *Finney*, 437 U.S. 678 (1978). The *Monell* Court overruled *Monroe* v. *Pape*, 365 U.S. 167 (1961), and held that units of local government are liable for damages in connection with constitutional violations committed by their employees pursuant to an official policy or custom. But, the Court added, local governments are not answerable for damages in connection with the constitutional torts of their employees that lack any official blessing or sponsorship. And a municipality might be entitled to some form of qualified immunity, the Court stated, even when sponsorship is demonstrated.

In *Hutto*, the Court held that states may be ordered to pay the plaintiff's attorneys' fees under the Civil Rights Attorney's Fees Awards Act of 1976 in suits brought to vindicate constitutional rights. In addition, *Hutto* affirmed a district court order placing a maximum limit of thirty days' confinement in punitive isolation as a partial remedy for unconstitutional living conditions that infected a state's penal institutions.

Although *Economou, Monell,* and *Hutto* removed some barriers to challenging unconstitutional action, *Stump* v. *Sparkman*, 435 U.S. 349 (1978), and *Procunier* v. *Navarette*, 434 U.S. 555 (1978), revealed that the obstacles that remain are formidable. In *Stump*, the Court held that the approval by a state judge of a mother's petition to sterilize her minor daughter, even if the approval was inspired by a malicious intent to violate the daughter's constitutional rights, offered no basis for a damage suit against the judge. Writing for a 5–3 majority, Justice White declared that judicial acts, no matter how wrongful, cannot expose a judge to damages unless they are taken in the "clear absence of all jurisdiction." An act is "judicial," White noted, if it is ordinarily performed by a judge and is taken at the behest of parties who deal with the judge in his judicial capacity. Applying these standards, White concluded that the defendant judge had power to entertain the sterilization petition and that his endorsement of the petition was a judicial act. Thus, the approval of the petition offered no foundation for liability for damages.

In *Procunier*, the Court held that 42 U.S. Code 1983 offered no remedy for damages to a prisoner who alleged that state prison officials had negligently interfered with his constitutional right to correspond by mail in failing to send various letters. Remedy for damages would be available, the Court explained, only if the defendants knew or reasonably should have known that their challenged conduct violated clearly established constitutional rights. The complaint was fatally defective, the Court concluded, because prisoners lacked any clearly established constitutional right to correspond by mail at the time the questioned conduct of the defendants occurred. State officials, the Court stressed, cannot be exposed to damages for failing to predict the future course of constitutional jurisprudence.

If a plaintiff succeeds in penetrating the formidable immunities offered government officials for constitutional torts, disputes over remedies frequently arise. Plaintiffs had little cause to celebrate the guidance offered to resolve such disputes in *Carey* v. *Piphus,* 435 U.S. 247 (1978), and *Robertson* v. *Wegmann,* 436 U.S. 584 (1978). In *Carey,* the Court addressed the question of how damages should be calculated under 42 U.S. Code 1983 after a constitutional violation has been proved. The remedy for damages offered by section 1983, said the Court, is intended to compensate for actual injuries, not to deter constitutional misdeeds. Common-law tort rules should be used, the Court concluded, as the starting point for determining whether a constitutional violation affords any basis for a recovery for damages. Applying these principles, the Court held that a violation of a student's procedural due process rights before his suspension from school would justify damages only if adherence to procedural due process would have exonerated the student or if he suffered mental or emotional distress on account of the procedural deficiencies.

In *Robertson,* the Court confronted the question of when state law should be applied in section 1983 suits to decide issues not addressed by the federal statute. A section 1983 plaintiff died while the suit was pending, and the executor of his estate moved to be substituted as plaintiff in a Louisiana federal district court. Section 1983 is silent on the question of whether the death of the plaintiff causes the action to abate, and 42 U.S. Code 1988 instructs federal courts to apply state law where federal law is deficient regarding suitable remedies if the state law would not frustrate federal statutory or constitutional policies. The relevant Louisiana survivorship statute permitted spouses, children, parents, or siblings, but not executors, to pursue the claims of a deceased litigant. Because the state survivorship statute was reasonably broad, reflected no hostility toward section 1983 actions generally, and offered no significant incentive to disregard constitutional restraints, the Court held that section 1988 required application of state law and thus the abatement of the lawsuit.

Procedural Due Process. The Fifth and Fourteenth amendments require adherence to procedures that satisfy due process if persons are deprived of constitutionally protected interests in liberty or property as a consequence of government action. Procedural due process, however, is not a procrustean concept. It is responsive to the conflicting concerns for individual rights and the needs of government. In *Ma-*

thews v. *Eldridge,* 424 U.S. 319 (1976), the Court identified three factors as the touchstone of procedural due process analysis:

First, the private interest that will be affected by the official action; second, the risk of an erroneous deprivation of such interest through the procedures used, and the probable value, if any, of additional or substitute procedural safeguards; and finally, the Government's interest, including the function involved and the fiscal and administrative burdens that additional or substitute procedural requirements would entail.

Of course, due process is required only when the private interest affected is entitled to constitutional protection and its deprivation may be ascribed to state action as opposed to private conduct.

In a trio of decisions this term, the Court voiced both sympathy and hostility toward procedural due process claims. Customers of municipal utilities are deprived of a constitutionally protected property interest, said the Court in *Memphis Light, Gas and Water Division* v. *Craft,* 436 U.S. 1 (1978), when gas and electric service are terminated for alleged nonpayment. Procedural due process, the Court held, requires municipal utilities to notify customers of any threatened termination for nonpayment and the availability of administrative procedures for challenging a disputed bill. In addition, before any termination, the customer must be given an opportunity to present any complaint to a designated employee who is empowered to review disputed bills and rectify error.

In contrast to a warm reception in *Memphis Light,* procedural due process claims were given a cold shoulder in *Board of Curators of the University of Missouri* v. *Horowitz,* 435 U.S. 78 (1978), and *Flagg Bros., Inc.* v. *Brooks,* 436 U.S. 149 (1978). In *Horowitz,* the Court was skeptical of the view that a state medical student, dismissed for failure to meet academic standards, had been deprived of a constitutionally protected liberty. Without resolving that issue, the Court ruled unanimously that the procedures followed by a state medical school in dismissing a student satisfied whatever due process would have required. The student was provided notice of dissatisfaction with her clinical progress and an opportunity to remedy her deficiencies. Dismissal was ordered only after a review of the student's clinical skills by seven independent physicians had confirmed a continuing failure to meet academic standards. Revealing its distaste for due process claims within the academic community, the Court declared: "We decline to further enlarge the judicial presence in the academic community and thereby risk deterioration of many beneficial aspects of the faculty-student relationship."

In *Flagg Bros.*, due process protections were curtailed by a crabbed application of the state-action doctrine. At issue was whether a provision of the New York Uniform Commercial Code (UCC) empowering a warehouseman to sell goods entrusted to him for storage to enforce a lien implicated the state in the warehouseman's action. Writing for a 5-3 majority, Justice Rehnquist explained that since a state does not monopolize the rights and remedies of debtors and creditors, it cannot invariably be held responsible for self-help remedies of the type permitted by the UCC. In addition, Rehnquist observed, the questioned statute neither compelled nor encouraged warehousemen to exercise self-help remedies. It merely defined the circumstances in which a private sale to enforce a lien could be made without threat of judicial interference. If a wrongful sale occurs, he noted, a remedy for damages is available. Accordingly, Rehnquist declared, a warehouseman's sale to enforce a lien as permitted by the UCC cannot be ascribed to state action and thus can escape the procedural encumbrances imposed by the Fourteenth Amendment.

Discrimination in Employment. In recent years there has been an unrelenting growth of female employees in the labor market.[6] Concurrently, an increasing number of employment practices have been attacked as sexually discriminatory under Title VII of the 1964 Civil Rights Act. In *Nashville Gas Co.* v. *Satty*, 434 U.S. 136 (1977), Title VII was invoked to upset an employer's practice of denying accumulated seniority to females returning to work following mandatory leaves of absence for childbirth. Seniority was retained and continued to accrue during leaves of absence taken for any other reason. The result of the employer's policy was to visit a permanent competitive disadvantage with respect to seniority solely on a class of female employees who took leave for childbirth. In the absence of a proven business necessity for such sex discrimination, the Court declared, it could not withstand Title VII scrutiny. The Court, however, adhered to its reasoning in *General Electric Co.* v. *Gilbert*, 429 U.S. 125 (1976), by declining to find any sex-based discrimination in the employer's sick-pay policy that compensated for disabilities attributable to nonoccupational sickness or injury but not those traceable to pregnancy. That policy, said the Court, erects no gender-based discrimination; it distinguishes between pregnant and nonpregnant persons, both of which classes include females. Accordingly, the Court held, it did not run afoul of the Title VII injunction against sex discrimi-

---

[6] The number of females in the labor force has grown during the past decade from approximately 28.5 million to 42.5 million, an increase of approximately 50 percent.

nation. Spurred by the rulings in *General Electric* and *Satty*, the 95th Congress enacted legislation that sharply curtails an employer's right to discriminate on the basis of pregnancy.[7]

The decision in *City of Los Angeles* v. *Manhart*, 435 U.S. 702 (1978), revealed the enormous potency of Title VII. There it was used to condemn a municipal pension plan that required female employees to contribute 15 percent more than their male counterparts because of their greater average longevity after retirement. The Court acknowledged that women as a class live longer than men and that female retirees as a class exact a larger drain on a pension fund than the class of male retirees. Nevertheless, it explained, Title VII requires that female employees be evaluated individually, not on the basis of general characteristics of their class. Since some female employees will not outlive their male counterparts, Title VII could not tolerate exacting higher pension contributions from every female. The Court emphasized, however, that its decision would permit an employer to set aside equal retirement contributions for each employee and let each retiree purchase the largest pension benefit which his or her accumulated contributions could command in the open market.

The *Manhart* decision may spur the insurance industry to develop unisex actuarial tables or benefit plans with unisex rates. It also casts grave doubt on the legality of "defined contribution" plans that award higher monthly retirement payments to male retirees than to female because of the shorter life expectancy of the former.

The aged who view compulsory retirement as their bête noire were dealt a severe setback in *United Air Lines, Inc.* v. *McMann*, 434 U.S. 192 (1977). A 7–2 majority of the Court ruled that the Age Discrimination in Employment Act of 1967 offered no protection against mandatory retirement at the age of sixty under a plan adopted years before the remedial legislation was enacted. The defeat, however, touched a responsive chord in Congress. It amended the 1967 act to overturn the *United Air Lines* decision and widen its protective ambit for aged employees.[8] Generally speaking, the amendments offer employees a shield against compulsory retirement because of age before seventy, with certain exceptions for professors and highly-paid executive officers. Federal employees are generally granted wholesale immunity from mandatory retirement on the basis of age.

A confrontation over employment on the Trans-Alaska Pipeline provided the backdrop for the decision in *Hicklin* v. *Orbeck*, 437 U.S.

---

[7] Act of October 31, 1978, P.L. 95–555, 92 Stat. 2076 (1978).
[8] Age Discrimination in Employment Act Amendments of 1978, P.L. 95–256, 92 Stat. 189 (1978).

518 (1978). By statute, Alaska commanded that qualified residents be preferred over nonresidents in filling jobs that were the offspring of oil-and-gas leases or easements for oil-and-gas pipelines to which the state was a party. A unanimous Court condemned the employment preference under the privileges and immunities clause of Article IV, Section 2. That clause establishes a norm of comity that enjoins states from preferring residents over nonresidents absent some compelling justification. The hiring preference, the Court said, was insufficiently geared to reducing state unemployment to satisfy the privileges and immunities clause. In addition, the Court emphasized, the preference was not confined to jobs created by the exploitation of gas-and-oil resources owned by the state; it was also extended to innumerable jobs attributable to the economic-ripple effect of this exploitation.

In recent years, aliens have wielded the equal protection clause to pry open opportunities for employment in the legal profession,[9] in the state[10] and federal[11] civil service, and in civil engineering.[12] This series of victories was broken by *Foley* v. *Connelie*, 435 U.S. 291 (1978), in which the Court sustained a state law that excluded aliens from the police force. The police function, the Court explained, is a central responsibility of government that requires the exercise of broad discretionary powers that may affect individuals in significant respects. Police officers, the Court continued, execute important public policies in their law-enforcement activities. Since such policies are derived from the political community's right to govern, the Court concluded, their execution may constitutionally be reserved to citizens.

Regents of the University of California v. *Bakke*, 438 U.S. 265 (1978)

Facts: A California state medical school adopted a special admissions program to increase the representation of "disadvantaged" students in each medical class. Sixteen places in an entering class of one hundred were set aside for blacks, chicanos, or Asians for admission under less exacting objective educational standards than were applied to the remaining eighty-four places. Allan Bakke, a white male, was denied admission to the medical school solely because his race disqualified him for competing with minorities for one of the sixteen reserved positions. He brought suit in state court contending

---

[9] In re Griffiths, 413 U.S. 717 (1973).
[10] Sugarman v. Dougall, 413 U.S. 634 (1973).
[11] Hampton v. Wong, 426 U.S. 88 (1976).
[12] Examining Board v. Flores de Otero, 426 U.S. 572 (1976).

that the program offended both the equal protection clause of the Fourteenth Amendment and Title VI of the Civil Rights Act of 1964. The trial court agreed, finding that the special program operated as a racial quota because it reserved sixteen places for minority applicants who would be rated only against one another. Relying solely on the equal protection clause, the Supreme Court of California generally affirmed the trial court's decision, ordered Bakke admitted to the medical school, and enjoined it from considering race in processing applications for admission.

Questions: (1) Did the special admissions program offend Title VI of the Civil Rights Act of 1964? (2) Did the program offend the equal protection clause of the Fourteenth Amendment? (3) Did the Supreme Court of California properly order Bakke's admission to the medical school? (4) Did the Supreme Court of California err in holding that the equal protection clause prohibits the medical school from giving positive weight to the race of a minority applicant in its admissions decisions?

Decision: Yes to question 1. No decision on question 2. Yes to questions 3 and 4. Plurality opinion by Justice Powell. Opinions concurring in part by Justices Brennan and Stevens. A majority of the Court ruled in favor of Bakke, but failed to agree on a rationale. Four justices rested their pro-Bakke votes on Title VI of the Civil Rights Act and were joined by Powell, whose vote rested on the equal protection clause.

Voting Alignments: Question 1: 5–4, Stevens, Burger, Rehnquist, Stewart, and Powell in the majority, Brennan, White, Blackmun, and Marshall dissenting. Question 2: 4–1, Brennan, White, Blackmun, and Marshall in the plurality, voting no, Powell in the minority, voting yes. Stevens, Burger, Rehnquist, and Stewart declined to reach the constitutional issue presented. Question 3: 5–4, Stevens, Burger, Rehnquist, Stewart, and Powell in the majority, Brennan, White, Blackmun, and Marshall dissenting. Question 4: 5–0, Powell, Brennan, White, Blackmun, and Marshall in the majority. Stevens, Burger, Rehnquist, and Stewart declined to reach the constitutional issue presented.

Plurality Opinion of Justice Powell: Title VI prohibits any program that receives federal financial assistance, including, it has been conceded, the medical school's admissions program, from discriminating on account of race. Legislative history demonstrates that this nondiscrimination principle condemns only racial classifications prohibited by the equal protection clause or the due process clause of the Fifth Amendment.

The special admissions program embraced a racial classification because it excluded all whites from competing for sixteen seats in the entering medical class. Distinctions among citizens that are founded solely on race, whether inspired by benign or invidious motives, are odious to a free people and are viewed with suspicion under the equal protection clause. Benign discrimination must be held to strict equal protection scrutiny because it may reinforce common stereotypes, force innocent persons to shoulder the burdens of redressing grievances not of their making, and disadvantage certain individuals within the protected racial class. Accordingly, the special admissions program satisfies equal protection scrutiny only if it is necessary in order to advance a compelling and legitimate government interest.

The medical school proffers four justifications to sustain the program: (1) increasing the number of traditionally disfavored minorities in medical schools and the medical profession, (2) countering the effects of societal discrimination, (3) increasing the number of practicing physicians in underserved communities, and (4) enriching the educational environment by assuring an ethnically diverse student body.

The first purpose is to increase minority representation in the medical community solely for its own sake and is an objective the Constitution will not countenance.

The second purpose is constitutionally legitimate: to ameliorate the disabling effects of identified discrimination. But to justify preferences to the injured racial class that disadvantage other races, there must be "judicial, legislative, or administrative findings" of unconstitutional or otherwise illegal discrimination. "After such findings have been made, the governmental interest in preferring members of the injured groups at the expense of others is substantial, since the legal rights of the victims must be vindicated." In this case, however, the medical school lacked both the capability and the authority to make findings of illegal discrimination against minorities. Its special admissions program cannot be sustained as a necessary remedy for mere perceptions of societal discrimination.

The third goal of the program—the improvement of health care in underserved communities—may be a compelling one. But the record is barren of evidence to show that setting aside sixteen places for minorities would have any significant effect on the problem or that minorities would be more likely than whites to serve in medically deprived communities.

The fourth goal—attaining a diverse student body in an institution of higher education—is constitutionally permissible. To achieve this goal, a school may give some preference to individuals from ethnic groups to obtain an ethnically diverse enrollment. Ethnic diversity, like geographic or cultural diversity, may bring experiences, outlooks, and ideas to a school that enrich the training and understanding of its student body and better equip its graduates to serve the community.

The constitutional flaw in the special admissions program is that it furthers diversity that is *solely* ethnic rather than the broader type of genuine diversity that may enrich the educational experience. The broader diversity that furthers a compelling interest embraces considerations of personal talents and background, leadership, compassion, diligence, culture, and ties with the poor as well as race. It permits each applicant to be considered as an individual, while giving a positive factor, but not a controlling one, to applicants of particular races. If the positive factor were intentionally weighted to achieve a racial quota, however, the admissions program would be constitutionally infirm.

In sum, the fatal vice in the special admissions program is that it disregards individual rights as guaranteed by the Fourteenth Amendment. It prevents whites, no matter what their individual potential for contributing to educational diversity, from competing with blacks, chicanos, and Asians for a specified percentage of seats in an entering medical class.

Opinion of Justice Stevens Concurring in Part and Joined by Burger, Rehnquist, and Stewart: Resolution of constitutional issues should be avoided if a case can be fairly decided on a statutory ground. Legislative history demonstrates persuasively that Title VI of the 1964 Civil Rights Act invalidates any racial classification that would exclude anyone from participation in a federally funded program. It is equally clear that Title VI offers a private cause of action to victims of such racial discrimination. Accordingly, Allan Bakke is entitled to enter the state medical school under the umbrella of Title VI, and the Court is not obligated to decide whether the Constitution would mandate the identical result.

Opinion of Justice Brennan Concurring in Part and Joined by White, Blackmun, and Marshall: The history of Title VI of the 1964 Civil Rights Act demonstrates that it forbids only those racial classifications that violate the equal protection clause. That clause does not view all such classifications with suspicion, at least those that do not demean or insult any racial group. Racial classifications designed to further remedial purposes pass equal protection scrutiny if they serve important government objectives and are substantially related to achievement of those objectives.

The special admissions program was intended to remedy past societal discrimination against minorities. Even in the absence of formal findings of discrimination, this objective was sufficiently important to justify use of race in processing applications for admission. Setting aside sixteen of a hundred seats solely for minorities was substantially related to overcoming handicaps inflicted by past and present racial discrimination. A single admissions standard would not have cured underrepresentation of minorities in the medical community because minorities continue to bear the lingering effects of historical educational discrimination. Likewise, a special admissions program tailored to benefit the socially or economically disadvantaged would have been futile because whites far outnumber minorities at every socioeconomic level.

Without stigmatizing any discrete group or individual, the contested admissions program legitimately gave preference to minority applicants likely to have been isolated from the mainstream of American life. The program is not vulnerable to equal protection challenge simply because it may benefit a few minorities who have escaped the effects of racial discrimination or because a predetermined number of places were set aside for qualified minorities.

> There is no sensible, and certainly no constitutional distinction between . . . adding a set number of points to the admissions rating of disadvantaged minority applicants [as Justice Powell would permit] as an expression of preference [for minorities] with the expectation that this will result in the admission of an approximately determined number of qualified minority applicants and setting a fixed number of places for such applicants [as Justice Powell condemned].

Butz v. *Economou*, 438 U.S. 478 (1978)

Facts: Seeking damages for alleged violations of several constitutional rights, a dealer in commodity futures sued the secretary of agriculture and the assistant secretary, administrative agency judicial officers, and a government attorney, among others. The foundation of the complaint was that these officials of the executive branch had knowingly authorized, prosecuted, and adjudicated a groundless administrative complaint charging the trader with failure to maintain minimum financial requirements prescribed by the department of agriculture. Relying on *Barr* v. *Matteo*, 360 U.S. 564 (1959), the district court dismissed the complaint on the ground that the defendants were absolutely immune to damage suits founded on acts that are within the scope of their authority. Reversing, the court of appeals held that officials of the executive branch enjoy only a qualified immunity from damage suits in which vindication of constitutional rights is sought. The immunity could be invoked, the court of appeals concluded, only if the contested actions were undertaken in good faith and with reasonable grounds to believe that they were constitutional.

Questions: (1) Are federal executive officials generally entitled to only a qualified immunity from damage suits founded on alleged violations of constitutional rights? (2) Are some executive officers blessed with absolute immunity in order to forestall harassment and intimidation of those involved in the prosecution and adjudication of administrative complaints?

Decision: Yes to both questions. Opinion by Justice White. Vote: 5–4, Rehnquist, Burger, Stewart, and Stevens dissenting on question 1.

Reasons: Past decisions expounding the immunity from damage suits enjoyed by federal executive officials do not point in one direction. In *Spalding* v. *Vilas*, 161 U.S. 483 (1896), and *Barr* v. *Matteo*, 360 U.S. 564 (1959), the Court held that executive officers were absolutely immune from common-law tort liability founded on conduct undertaken within the range of their lawful authority. On the other hand, *Bivens* v. *Six Unknown Named Agents of the Federal Bureau of Narcotics*, 403 U.S. 388 (1971), implied that such officers were entitled to only a qualified immunity to damages brought about by constitutional transgressions. Principles of justice and the qualified immunity of state officials to damage suits under 42 U.S. Code 1983 justify embracing the implication of *Bivens*.

The touchstone of civil liberty is the right of individuals to claim the protection of the laws. When personal interests in liberty have been unlawfully invaded, damage suits have been regarded as the ordinary remedy. This damage remedy, however, must at times be subordinated to the greater public interest in attracting highly qualified persons to government service who will execute their duties with decisiveness and vigor. In granting state executive officers a qualified immunity to damage suits that arise form constitutional torts under section 1983, the Court in *Scheuer* v. *Rhodes*, 416 U.S. 232 (1974), relied on the injustice, in the absence of bad faith, of exposing an officer to liability for exercising discretion, and the danger that the threat of such liability would beget a timid execution of his office. An absolute immunity, *Scheuer* concluded, however, would unduly denigrate the interests of individuals in redressing constitutional injuries inflicted maliciously or in bad faith.

> [I]n the absence of congressional direction to the contrary, there is no basis for according to federal officials a higher degree of immunity from liability when sued for a constitutional infringement . . . than is accorded state officials when sued for the identical violation under section 1983. . . . The pressures and uncertainties facing decisionmakers in state government are little if at all different from those affecting federal officials. . . . To create a system in which the Bill of Rights monitors more closely the conduct of state officials than it does that of federal officials is to stand the constitutional design on its head.

There are exceptional situations, however, in which "absolute" immunity is essential for the conduct of the public business" and may be invoked by federal or state officials. In *Pierson* v. *Ray*, 386 U.S. 547 (1967), and *Imbler* v. *Pachtman*, 424 U.S. 409 (1976), judges and prosecutors were offered absolute immunity to forestall threats to fair adjudication and effective law enforcement that could be engendered by exposing such officers to damage suits brought by angry or dissatisfied litigants. Adjudication within a federal administrative agency is sufficiently similar to the judicial process to justify cloaking its participants with absolute immunity. The powers, independence, and impartiality of the federal hearing examiner or administrative law judge closely resemble those of a trial judge. Agency officials who authorize the initiation of administrative complaints exercise a discretion comparable to that of a prosecutor. And an agency attorney who conducts a trial and presents evidence in an administrative proceeding mirrors the role of a prosecuting attorney in a criminal case. The adjudicative and prosecutorial judgments of these executive officers would be distorted if they faced the threat of intimidation or harassment through actions that challenge the propriety of their official decisions.

Monell v. *Department of Social Services of the City of New York*, 436 U.S. 658 (1978)

Facts: Seeking back pay, female employees sued the department of social services, the board of education, the city of New York, and various individuals in their official capacities under 42 U.S. Code 1983. The complaint alleged that the official policy of the department and the board compelled pregnant employees to take medically unnecessary unpaid leaves of absence in contravention of the due process clause. Granting summary judgment for the defendants, the district court reasoned that any award of damages would be paid by the city of New York and was therefore barred by *Monroe* v. *Pape*, 365 U.S. 167 (1961). There the Court held that section 1983 offered no protection against municipalities that violated constitutional rights. The court of appeals affirmed.

Question: Should *Monroe* v. *Pape* be overruled insofar as it shields local governing bodies from suit under section 1983 when official policies or customs offend constitutional norms?

Decision: Yes. Opinion by Justice Brennan. Vote: 7–2, Stevens concurring in part, Rehnquist and Burger dissenting.

Reasons: Section 1983 creates a cause of action against "[a]ny person" who, acting under color of state law, directly or indirectly causes a deprivation of constitutional rights. In *Monroe* v. *Pape*, the Court clearly misinterpreted legislative history in holding that Congress intended to exclude municipalities wholesale from liability under section 1983. Congressional rejection of the so-called Sherman amendment to the statute before its enactment—the foundation of the *Monroe* decision—reflected an intent to shield municipalities lacking law enforcement powers from liability for the riotous actions of residents that violated constitutional rights. The overwhelming weight of additional legislative materials and appropriate rules of statutory construction confirm the view that Congress did intend to expose municipalities and other units of local government to liability under section 1983 in some circumstances.

> Local governing bodies . . . can be sued directly under section 1983 for monetary, declaratory, or injunctive relief where, as here, the action that is alleged to be unconstitutional implements or executes a policy statement, ordinance, regulation, or decision officially adopted and promulgated by that body's officers. Moreover . . . local governments . . . may be sued for constitutional deprivations visited pursuant to governmental "custom" even though such a custom has not received formal approval through the body's official decisionmaking channels.

The defeat of the Sherman amendment and the language of section 1983, however, manifest an intent to deny municipal liability founded solely on the theory that a municipal employee committed a constitutional tort—"or, in other words a municipality cannot be held liable under section 1983 on a *respondent superior* theory."

Several reasons justify departing from *stare decisis* and overruling *Monroe*. First, its holding was inconsistent with earlier decisions. Second, Congress has recently attempted to confine the immunity offered by *Monroe* to municipalities. Third, no municipality could legitimately violate constitutional rights in reliance on *Monroe*. Finally, it is "beyond doubt" that section 1983 was construed erroneously in *Monroe*.

The Court expresses no view as to whether local government bodies are entitled to some form of qualified immunity under section 1983.

Hutto v. *Finney*, 437 U.S. 678 (1978)

Facts: A federal district court found that conditions in the Arkansas penal system offended the Eighth Amendment prohibition against cruel and unusual punishment. One of its remedial orders placed a maximum limit of thirty days on confinement in punitive isolation. In addition, after finding that Arkansas had acted in bad faith in failing to cure previously identified constitutional violations, the district court awarded attorneys' fees of the plaintiffs to be paid by the state. The court of appeals affirmed, and, relying on the Civil Rights Attorney's Fees Awards Act of 1976, awarded plaintiffs an additional $2,500 to cover fees and expenses on appeal.

Questions: Were (1) the order limiting confinement of inmates in punitive isolation and (2) the district court order and (3) the court of appeals order assessing attorneys' fees against the state beyond constitutional or statutory reproach?

Decision: Yes to each question. Opinion by Justice Stevens. Votes: 8–1, 7–2, and 5–4, respectively, Rehnquist dissenting on questions 1, 2, and 3, White dissenting on questions 2 and 3, Powell and Burger dissenting on question 3.

Reasons: The district court found that Arkansas's use of indeterminate sentences to punitive isolation, when combined with filth, overcrowding, and insufficient diet, offended the Eighth Amendment as made applicable to the states by the Fourteenth Amendment. A thirty-day maximum limit on this type of punishment was necessary to ensure against risk of inadequate compliance with previous orders to remedy the cruel and unusual conditions in the isolated cells. In light of the state's history of recalcitrance, the thirty-day limit was justified. It threatens little or no interference with prison administration, since the state has conceded that punitive isolation should not ordinarily be used for more than fourteen days.

The state urges that the Eleventh Amendment prohibited the award of attorneys' fees by the district court. While shielding states from retroactive monetary relief, the amendment is impotent against injunctions of a federal court and remedial fines designed to punish noncompliance with prospective relief. The contested award of attorneys' fees for litigating in bad faith was intended to secure state compliance with the district court's outstanding decree that was fashioned to eliminate unconstitutional prison conditions. "We see no reason to distinguish this award from any other penalty imposed to enforce a prospective injunction."

The assessment of attorneys' fees against the state by the court of appeals was authorized by the Civil Rights Attorney's Fees Awards Act, 42 U.S. Code 1988. Its legislative history evinces an intent to remove any Eleventh Amendment immunity that states would otherwise enjoy against damage recoveries awarded by federal courts. The power of Congress to abrogate this immunity in suits against states that vindicate constitutional rights was acknowledged in *Fitzpatrick* v. *Bitzer*, 427 U.S. 455 (1976). Although the express language of the act omits reference to abrogation of state immunity, that omission is not fatal to holding states liable for awards of attorneys' fees. The rationale of *Fairmont Creamery Co.* v. *Minnesota*, 275 U.S. 70 (1927), permits Congress to authorize an award of attorney's fees as an item of the cost of litigation against a state without using express statutory language to that effect.

Stump v. *Sparkman*, 435 U.S. 349 (1978)

Facts: In an *ex parte* proceeding, a mother petitioned an Indiana state judge to authorize the sterilization of her "somewhat retarded" fifteen-year-old daughter, as a condition of which she agreed to indemnify the doctor and hospital involved in performing the operation against any lawsuits that it might trigger. The state judge approved the petition in a document that he signed as "Judge, Dekalb Circuit Court." Two years after her sterilization, the daughter sued the judge for damages under 42 U.S. Code 1983 alleging that his approval of the petition violated several constitutional rights. The district court ruled that the judge was clothed with absolute immunity for his questioned conduct, but the court of appeals reversed. It held that judicial immunity under section 1983 was forfeited whenever a state judge acted beyond his jurisdiction or defied elementary principles of procedural due process.

Question: Was the state judge absolutely immune from liability for damages under section 1983 for approving the petition seeking authorization to sterilize the daughter?

Decision: Yes. Opinion by Justice White. Vote: 5–3, Stewart, Marshall, and Powell dissenting. Brennan did not participate.

Reasons: Section 1983 authorizes damage suits against "any person" who violates another's constitutional rights under color of state law. Despite its sweeping language, the statute was not intended to strip state officials of immunities that they enjoyed under common law. In *Pierson* v. *Ray,* 386 U.S. 547 (1967), the Court held that section 1983 embraced the common-law rule that state judges cannot be made to answer in damages for their judicial acts, even when such acts are in excess of their jurisdiction and were committed maliciously or corruptly. Judicial immunity lapses only when a judge acts in the "clear absence of all jurisdiction."

In this case, the state judge had "original exclusive jurisdiction in all cases at law and in equity whatsoever" and over "all other causes, matters and proceedings where exclusive jurisdiction thereof is not conferred by law upon some other court, board or officer." Although no Indiana statute expressly provides for judicial approval of sterilization petitions, when the state judge acted there was no clear and unambiguous authority to the contrary. Accordingly, the judge's consideration of the petition for sterilization was not clearly foreclosed by Indiana law; it was thus clothed with immunity whether or not the judge's action in approving the petition was replete with grave procedural errors and otherwise erroneous as a matter of law.

The contention that the approval of the petition was not a "judicial" act and thus fell outside the protection of judicial immunity is unfounded. Generally speaking, judicial acts are those normally performed by a judge and spring from situations in which parties have dealt with the judge in his judicial capacity. The questioned petition was akin to those related to the affairs of minors over which the defendant state judge had general jurisdiction. In addition, the petition, was presented and acted upon by the judge in his judicial capacity.

Because [the state judge] performed the type of act normally performed only by judges and because he did so in his capacity as a circuit court judge, we find no merit . . . [in the] argument that the informality with which he proceeded rendered his action nonjudicial and deprived him of his absolute immunity.

Procunier v. *Navarette*, 434 U.S. 555 (1978)

Facts: A prison inmate sued several prison officials for damages under 42 U.S. Code 1983 alleging, *inter alia,* that their negligent failure to mail many of his letters between September 1971 and December 1972 violated his constitutional rights to free speech and due process. The district court granted summary judgment for the prison officials on the ground that they enjoyed qualified immunity from liability under section 1983. The court of appeals reversed, reasoning that the evidence most favorable to the prisoner's damage claim did not foreclose the possibility of recovery as a matter of law.

Question: Did the court of appeals err in overturning the district court's grant of summary judgment?

Decision: Yes. Opinion by Justice White. Vote: 7–2, Burger and Stevens dissenting.

Reasons: Prior decisions clearly establish that section 1983 did not strip state officials of whatever common-law immunity they enjoyed from damage suits. With this understanding, section 1983 should be construed to clothe prison officials, like other executive or administrative officers, with a qualified immunity from liability for damages. As the Court explained in *Wood* v. *Strickland*, 420 U.S. 308 (1975), this damage shield could not be pierced unless a state official either acted with a malicious intent to deprive another of his constitutional rights or knew or reasonably should have known that his questioned conduct offended constitutional norms.

Under the first part of the *Wood* v. *Strickland* liability rule, the prisoner's quest for damages under section 1983 was unavailing because he alleged only negligent, not malicious, interference with his constitutional rights. Relief for damages was likewise unavailable under the second part of the rule. In 1971 and 1972, prisoners could point to no clearly established constitutional right to send correspondence to outsiders. Indeed, in 1974, the Court specifically avoided resolving this question in *Procunier* v. *Martinez*, 416 U.S. 396, and it remains unresolved today. Accordingly, at the time of their conduct that was allegedly to have been offending, the prison officials could neither have known nor reasonably have been expected to anticipate the emergence of a constitutional right of inmates to correspond with outsiders. Liability for damages under section 1983 cannot be founded on the failure of state officials to predict the future development of constitutional jurisprudence.

Carey v. *Piphus*, 435 U.S. 247 (1978)

Facts: A principal summarily suspended two high school students whom he suspected of smoking marijuana in violation of a school rule. Thereafter, the principal was sued for damages under 42 U.S. Code 1983, on the theory that his failure to afford the students an opportunity for a hearing prior to the suspension offended procedural due process. An elementary school principal was also sued for damages under section 1983 on the identical theory for summarily suspending a male pupil who defied a school rule against wearing earrings. Concluding that the summary suspensions were constitutionally infirm, the district court declined to award damages because the students failed to prove that the lack of a hearing had caused them any injury. The court of appeals reversed, holding that denial of procedural due process triggers a right to substantial nonpunitive damages under section 1983, even when there is no proof of individual injury.

Question: In a section 1983 suit founded on a violation of procedural due process, must a plaintiff prove actual injury attributable to the violation before he may recover substantial nonpunitive damages?

Decision: Yes. Opinion by Justice Powell. Vote: 8–0, Marshall concurring in the result. Blackmun did not participate.

Reasons: The recovery for damages offered by section 1983 was intended to compensate persons for injuries caused by departures from constitutional norms; it was not crafted "to establish a deterrent more formidable than that inherent in the award of compensatory damages."

The common-law rules of damages applicable in tort law should guide the development of damage rules applicable to constitutional torts under section 1983. "[T]he rules governing compensation for injuries caused by the deprivation of constitutional rights should be tailored to the interests protected by the particular right in question." Procedural due process protections are meant to forestall unjustified deprivations of life, liberty, or property and to convey to individuals a feeling that government has dealt with them fairly. These purposes would not be offended if the school principals could prove that the suspensions in question would have been ordered even if proper hearings had been held and the students failed to prove any emotional or mental distress caused by the denial of procedural due process. Contrary to the view of the court of appeals, section 1983 does not justify a presumption of damages for every departure from procedural due process commands.

Despite the absence of actual injury, common-law courts have traditionally awarded nominal damages to vindicate certain absolute rights that, as society recognizes, should be scrupulously observed.

> Because the right to procedural due process is "absolute" in the sense that it does not depend upon the merits of a claimant's substantive assertions, and because of the importance to organized society that procedural due process be observed, we believe that the denial of procedural due process should be actionable for nominal damages [not to exceed one dollar] without proof of actual injury.

Robertson v. *Wegmann*, 436 U.S. 584 (1978)

Facts: Clay Shaw died while his damage suit against district attorney Jim Garrison and others, brought in a Louisiana federal court, was pending. Founded on 42 U.S. Code 1983, the complaint alleged that the defendants acted unconstitutionally and in bad faith in prosecuting Shaw for conspiracy to assassinate President Kennedy and for perjury on the basis of his testimony at the conspiracy trial. Opposing the motion of the executor of Shaw's estate to be substituted as a plaintiff, defendants sought dismissal of the suit, urging that under 42 U.S. Code 1988, Louisiana's survivorship statute should govern the question of whether substitution was appropriate. Under Louisiana law, Shaw's section 1983 action would survive in favor of a spouse, children, parents, or siblings, but not in favor of an executor. Concluding that federal law was deficient with respect to survivorship and that application of Louisiana law would offend the remedial purposes of section 1983, the district court permitted substitution, relying on its authority to create federal common law when it is necessary in order to vindicate federal policies. The court of appeals affirmed.

Question: Was it an error to disregard Louisiana's survivorship statute in determining whether Shaw's section 1983 action could be pursued by the executor of his estate?

Decision: Yes. Opinion by Justice Marshall. Vote: 6–3, Blackmun, Brennan, and White dissenting.

Reasons: When federal law fails to offer suitable remedies for section 1983 violations, 42 U.S. Code 1988 instructs federal courts to apply the applicable state law except when it is inconsistent with the Constitution or federal statutes. Since federal law fails to address the question of survival of section 1983 actions, the Louisiana survivorship statute should have been applied to provide the answer unless it would undermine either of the dual policies of section 1983: deterrence of constitutional violations and compensation to victims of constitutional misconduct. Louisiana's survivorship statute would not impair the compensatory purpose of section 1983, because the executor of Shaw's estate was not victimized by a constitutional violation. Neither would the statute undermine the goal of deterrence in this case, in which the alleged constitutional violation was not a cause of Shaw's death. A state official contemplating illegal activity must always be prepared to counter an action under section 1983, which in most cases will survive the victims' death under Louisiana law.

> Our holding today is a narrow one, limited to situations in which no claim is made that state law generally is inhospitable to survival of section 1983 actions and in which the particular application of state survivorship law, while it may cause abatement of the action, has no independent adverse effect on the policies underlying section 1983.

Memphis Light, Gas and Water Division v. *Craft,* 436 U.S. 1 (1978)

Facts: A municipal utility in Tennessee terminated the gas and electric service of a residential customer on five separate occasions for nonpayment. The customer was notified before each termination of service and discussed billing disputes with employees of the utility without satisfaction. Thereafter, the customer sued the utility under 42 U.S. Code 1983, alleging that the termination of his utility service deprived him of a property interest without the procedural due process safeguards mandated by the Fourteenth Amendment. The district court rendered judgment for the utility, but the court of appeals reversed. It reasoned that the customer had a constitutionally protected property interest in the continuance of gas and electric service and that the notice and hearing provided before its termination offended procedural due process. To satisfy due process, the court of appeals held, the utility must notify customers of the possibility of termination and of procedures for challenging a disputed bill and must establish a regular mechanism for resolving customer billing disputes.

Question: Did the court of appeals correctly discern the due process restraints on the municipal utility's right to terminate gas and electric service for nonpayment?

Decision: Yes. Opinion by Justice Powell. Vote: 6–3, Stevens, Burger, and Rehnquist dissenting.

Reasons: Tennessee law prohibits a public utility from terminating the service of a customer for nonpayment when a bona fide billing dispute exists. This protection offered the customer by state law is sufficiently weighty to create a property interest protected by the due process clause of the Fourteenth Amendment.

A fundamental dictate of due process is notice reasonably calculated to inform interested parties of prospective action and of an opportunity to present their objections. As applied to the municipal utility, due process requires that customers be informed of any prospective termination of service and of an avenue of redress within the organization that may be used to contest a particular charge.

The type of hearing demanded by due process before the deprivation of property interests generally turns on three factors: the importance of the private interest at stake; the risk of an erroneous deprivation of the interest through the questioned procedures; and the government interest in avoiding fiscal, administrative, and other burdens that additional procedural safeguards would entail. An evaluation of these concerns yields the conclusion that the utility must establish some regular administrative procedure for entertaining complaints of customers prior to the termination of service. Utility service is a necessity of modern life. The widespread use of computers in the billing process creates a substantial risk of erroneous termination for nonpayment if an opportunity for entertaining disputes with customers is not offered. And the utility will not be burdened by making a responsible employee, empowered to resolve billing disputes, available to complaining customers before termination. The utility would retain the right to terminate service after providing this informal hearing if it concluded that the amount billed was justly due.

The existence of state judicial remedies for improper termination of service does not answer the due process objections to the utility's procedures.

> Judicial remedies are particularly unsuited to the resolution of factual disputes typically involving sums of money too small to justify engaging counsel or bringing a lawsuit. An action in equity to halt an improper termination, because it is less likely to be pursued and less likely to be effective, even if pursued, will not provide the same assurance of accurate decisionmaking as would an adequate administrative procedure.

Board of Curators of the University of Missouri v. Horowitz, 435 U.S. 78 (1978)

Facts: A state medical school dismissed a student during her final year of study for failure to meet academic standards. Recommendations made by a student-faculty council on evaluation, seven practicing physicians who supervised the student's clinical studies, and a faculty review committee provided the foundation for the decision. Dismissal was recommended because the student's clinical skills and rapport with patients were unsatisfactory. Although the student had been both warned of her clinical deficiencies and offered an opportunity to improve her performance, no formal or informal hearing was provided before dismissal was ordered. The student brought suit in federal district court, alleging that the dismissal deprived her of liberty without due process of law by impairing her opportunities to continue her medical education and to obtain employment in medically related fields. The district court held that the procedures followed by the state medical school satisfied the due process command of the Fourteenth Amendment, but the court of appeals reversed.

Question: Did the dismissal of the state medical student for unsatisfactory academic performance violate the procedural due process requirements of the Fourteenth Amendment?

Decision: No. Opinion by Justice Rehnquist. Vote. 9–0, White concurring in part and concurring in the judgment, Marshall, Blackmun, and Brennan concurring in part and dissenting in part.

Reasons: It is unnecessary to decide whether the student's dismissal deprived her of a constitutionally protected liberty in pursuing a medical career. Assuming the existence of a liberty interest, the state medical school offered at least as many procedural safeguards as due process requires. The student was informed of her unsatisfactory clinical performance by independent physicians with firsthand knowledge of her work. Since the dismissal was prompted by academic evaluations of the student rather than alleged misconduct, no adversary hearing of any type was constitutionally required. Academic judgments are inherently more subjective and evaluative than the typical factual questions presented in the average disciplinary decision. Like the decision of an individual professor as to the proper grade for a student in his course, the determination whether to dismiss a student for academic reasons requires an expert evaluation of cumulative information and is not readily adapted to the procedural tools of judicial or administrative decisionmaking.

A prominent judicial presence in the academic community would jeopardize many beneficial aspects of the faculty-student relationship. Caution and restraint should guide federal courts in ruling on claims inviting judicial interposition in the operations of public education. This principle requires summary rejection of the additional contention that the student's dismissal was arbitrary and capricious and offended substantive due process, because no such showing of arbitrariness has been made.

Flagg Bros., Inc. v. *Brooks,* 436 U.S. 149 (1978)

Facts: A warehouseman is permitted under section 7–210 of the New York Uniform Commercial Code (UCC) to sell goods entrusted to him for storage in a commercially reasonable manner in order to enforce a lien on the goods that have arisen for nonpayment of storage charges. A tenant whose goods were stored by a warehouseman following her eviction from an apartment defaulted on her storage payments. To forestall a private sale of her belongings under the UCC, she brought suit under 42 U.S. Code 1983, claiming that the sale would offend the due process and equal protection clauses of the Fourteenth Amendment. The district court held the complaint deficient under section 1983 because of the absence of any state involvement in sales made pursuant to section 7–210. Reversing, the court of appeals ruled that a warehouseman's sale under that section was functionally identical to the duties traditionally performed by sheriffs in executing a lien and therefore constituted state action for purposes of the Fourteenth Amendment.

Question: Do sales made by warehousemen pursuant to section 7–210 constitute state action that is circumscribed by the due process and equal protection clauses of the Fourteenth Amendment?

Decision: No. Opinion by Justice Rehnquist. Vote: 5–3, Marshall, Stevens, and White dissenting. Brennan did not participate.

Reasons: Section 1983 offers protection against constitutional violations committed under color of state law. Accordingly, section 7–210 is invulnerable to attack under section 1983 unless sales by warehousemen to enforce liens can fairly be attributed to the state of New York. Two theories are advanced to justify such attribution.

First, it is urged that section 7–210 delegates a power that has traditionally been reserved exclusively to the state: the resolution of private contractual disputes. This argument is misconceived, because the invocation of section 7–210 was not the exclusive means of resolving the tenant's private dispute with her warehouseman. She might have sought a waiver of his section 7–210 rights at the time of storage or might have brought suit to replevy her goods under state law. A remedy for damages is available, moreover, if section 7–210 sales do not conform to its detailed safeguards. In short, "[t]his system of rights and remedies, recognizing the traditional place of private arrangements in ordering relationships in the commercial world, can hardly be said to have delegated to [warehousemen] an exclusive prerogative of the sovereign." Accordingly, decisions holding that state action is implicated in the private performance of exclusive public functions, such as the election of public officials or the operation of an entire municipality, do not justify attributing the action of a warehouseman under section 7–210 to the state.

It is also argued that sales under section 7–210 implicate the state because its laws authorize and encourage such action. State-action jurisprudence, however, has firmly disavowed the theory that "a State's mere acquiescence in a private action converts that action into that of the State." Here, section 7–210 does not compel private sales but merely announces the circumstances under which state courts will not interfere with their execution. The state's refusal to frustrate a purely private choice to invoke section 7–210 does not transform that choice into state action.

The Court expresses no view as to the extent, if any, to which a state may delegate to private parties such functions as education, fire and police protection, and tax collection and thereby avoid the strictures of the Fourteenth Amendment.

Nashville Gas Co. v. *Satty,* 434 U.S. 136 (1977)

Facts: A female employee claimed that two policies of the Nashville Gas Company unlawfully discriminated on the basis of sex in violation of Title VII of the Civil Rights Act of 1964, section 703(a)(2). The first denied accumulated seniority to female employees who returned to work following disability caused by childbirth. The second offered sick pay to employees whose disabilities arose from nonoccupational sickness or injury but not to those whose disabilities were the result of pregnancy. A federal court of appeals sustained both claims.

Question: Do the employment policies of the Nashville Gas Company that discriminate against pregnancy violate section 703(a)(2) of Title VII?

Decision: Yes with regard to the denial of accumulated seniority, and no with regard to sick-pay coverage. Opinion by Justice Rehnquist. Vote: 9–0, Powell, Brennan, and Marshall concurring in the result and concurring in part, Stevens concurring in the judgment.

Reasons: Section 703(a)(2) prohibits employers from classifying employees in any way that would "tend to deprive any individual of employment opportunities or otherwise adversely affect his status as an employee" on account of sex. Nashville Gas Company's seniority policy on its face establishes a classification based not on sex but on pregnancy. In *Griggs* v. *Duke Power Co.,* 401 U.S. 431 (1971), however, it was recognized that both intentional sex discrimination and policies having a sexually discriminatory impact may offend section 703(a)(2). Nashville Gas Company's policy of depriving employees returning from pregnancy leave of their accumulated seniority both deprives them of employment opportunities and adversely affects their employment status. This burden is borne only by female employees; males taking leaves of absence are not comparably penalized. Since Nashville Gas Company failed to prove any business necessity for embracing a seniority policy hostile to pregnancy, it must be condemned under section 703(a)(2).

The questioned sick-pay policy is legally indistinguishable from the disability insurance program that excluded pregnancy-related disabilities and obtained the Court's endorsement in *General Electric Co.* v. *Gilbert,* 429 U.S. 125 (1976). Nashville Gas Company compensates employees for limited periods when absences are caused by a non-job-related illness or disability, but not for pregnancy-related absences. There has been no showing, however, that Nashville Gas Company's sick-pay benefits in the aggregate work a discrimination against any definable group or class, or that the exclusion of pregnancy from the compensated conditions was a mere pretext for effecting an invidious discrimination against female employees. Under *Gilbert*, the lack of such evidence renders the attack on Nashville Gas Company's sick-pay policy fatally defective.

City of Los Angeles, Department of Water and Power v. *Manhart*, 435 U.S. 702 (1978)

Facts: Relying on actuarial tables in which it is shown that women as a class live longer than men, the Los Angeles Department of Water and Power required its female employees to contribute 15 percent more than comparable male employees to its pension fund. The enhanced contribution of female employees was necessary to offset the larger pension payments received by the class of female retirees as opposed to male retirees because of the greater longevity of the average female. Female employees brought suit, assailing the exaction of enhanced pension contributions under section 703(a)(1) of the 1964 Civil Rights Act as unlawful sex discrimination. The district court upheld the claim and ordered a refund of excess contributions. The court of appeals affirmed.

Questions: (1) Does section 703(a)(1) of the 1964 Civil Rights Act condemn pension plans that exact higher contributions from female employees than from male employees in order to offset the higher pension payments received by the average female retiree? (2) Should a refund of any excess contributions be ordered?

Decision: Yes to the first question and no to the second. Opinion by Justice Stevens. Votes: 6–2 and 7–1, respectively, Burger, Rehnquist, and Marshall concurring in part and dissenting in part, Blackmun concurring in part and concurring in the judgment. Brennan did not participate.

Reasons: Section 703(a)(1)makes it unlawful "to discriminate against any individual with respect to his compensation, terms, conditions, or privileges of employment, because of such individual's . . . sex." It prohibits treating an individual on the basis of generalizations applicable to a sexual class that are not universally true. The questioned contribution differential of female employees is flawed under section 703(a)(1) because there is no assurance that any individual female employee of the department will actually live longer than the average male employee. The females who die before the average male will have received smaller take-home pay because of their sex without any compensatory advantage in their pensions.

This interpretation of section 703(a)(1) may be unfair to the class of male employees because of the impossibility of determining which females will predecease the average woman while pension contributions are collected. Unless women as a class are assessed an extra charge, they will reap a subsidy from the class of male employees. The proper forum for airing such charges of unfairness, however, is Congress.

By condemning the department's pension plan under section 703(a)(1):

> we do not suggest that the statute was intended to revolutionize the insurance and pension industries. . . . Nothing in our holding implies that it would be unlawful for an employer to set aside equal retirement contributions for each employee and let each retiree purchase the largest benefit which his or her accumulated contributions could command in the open market. Nor does it call into question the insurance industry practice of considering the composition of an employer's work force in determining the probable cost of a retirement or death benefit plan.

The district court, however, erred in ordering a refund of the excess contributions at issue in this case. In *Albemarle Paper Co.* v. *Moody*, 422 U.S. 405 (1975), the Court held that violations of Title VII trigger a presumption in favor of retroactive liability. Nevertheless, several factors in this case clearly outweigh the presumption: the good faith of the department in establishing its contested pension plan; the threat to the actuarial soundness of insurance and pension plans affecting millions that retroactive liability would create; and the injury that retroactive liability would visit on innocent third parties.

United Air Lines, Inc. v. *McMann,* 434 U.S. 192 (1977)

Facts: In 1941, United Air Lines inaugurated a voluntary retirement income plan that required participants to retire at the age of sixty. A participating employee, aged sixty, objected to his compulsory retirement in 1973. He claimed that the provisions for retirement before the age of sixty-five violated the Age Discrimination in Employment Act of 1967. A federal court of appeals sustained the claim in part, holding that plans requiring retirement before the age of sixty-five run afoul of the act unless they are justified by economic or business purposes unrelated to arbitrary age discrimination.

Question: Does the Age Discrimination in Employment Act condemn plans adopted before its enactment that require retirement before the age of sixty-five unless the requirement furthers some economic or business purpose?

Decision: No. Opinion by Chief Justice Burger. Vote: 7–2, Stewart and White concurring in the judgment, Brennan and Marshall dissenting.

Reasons: The act protects persons between the ages of forty and sixty-five and makes it unlawful for an employer to discriminate against any individual in this class because of age. Section 4(f)(2) of the act shelters a bona fide retirement plan from challenge, however, unless it was embraced as a subterfuge to evade the purpose of the act: encouraging the employment of older persons on the basis of ability without respect to age. Legislative history reveals an intent to advance this goal by prohibiting discrimination against elderly applicants in hiring because their employment might engender relatively high retirement, pension, or insurance costs. But it also discloses endorsement of bona fide plans that call for retirement before the age of sixty-five unless they were adopted to circumvent the nondiscrimination goals of the statute.

> [A] plan established in 1941, if bona fide, as is conceded here, cannot be a subterfuge to evade an Act passed twenty-six years later. To spell out an intent in 1941 to evade a statutory requirement not enacted until 1967 attributes, at the very least, a remarkable prescience to the employer.

Hicklin v. *Orbeck,* 437 U.S. (1978)

Facts: Ostensibly for the purpose of reducing unemployment in Alaska, its legislature passed a statute in 1972 that mandated the employment of qualified residents of Alaska in preference to nonresidents on jobs stemming from oil and gas leases, easements for oil and gas pipelines, and unitization agreements to which the state is a party. Nonresidents denied employment on the Trans-Alaska pipeline project challenged the constitutionality of the employment preference under the privileges and immunities clause of Article IV,

Section 2. The Alaska Supreme Court rejected the attack except for a one-year residency requirement.

Question: Does the privileges and immunities clause condemn Alaska's statutory preference for residents over nonresidents in filling jobs stemming from oil and gas leases, oil and gas pipeline easements, and unitization agreements, to which the state is a party?

Decision: Yes. Opinion by Justice Brennan for a unanimous Court.

Reasons: The privileges and immunities clause establishes a norm of comity that sharply circumscribes the power of states to discriminate against nonresidents who are engaged in commercial endeavors. At a minimum, such discrimination can be justified only if nonresidents are the source of the evil that the state seeks to remedy. In this case, the evidence showed that Alaska's high unemployment reflected a lack of job skills among a large number of Indian and Eskimo residents, not an influx of nonresidents seeking employment. Accordingly, a high rate of unemployment offered no foundation for seeking to isolate Alaska's job market from nonresidents.

Alaska's discrimination against nonresidents is also constitutionally flawed because it lacks any "substantial relationship" to the unemployment problem. It grants all Alaskans an employment preference, whether or not they are disadvantaged, unskilled, or otherwise unlikely to succeed in a competitive market.

Finally, the preference cannot survive privileges and immunities scrutiny simply because the jobs that it protects for residents had some relationship to the state's ownership of oil and gas. The preference sweeps in all jobs offered by contractors, subcontractors, and their suppliers who have no contractual or other relationship with Alaska, its land, or its oil and gas. Although these employment opportunities may represent the economic-ripple effect of Alaska's decision to develop its oil and gas resources, the link between the two is too tenuous to justify Alaska's pervasive discrimination against nonresidents.

Foley v. Connelie, 435 U.S. 291 (1978)

Facts: A New York statute prohibits the appointment of aliens to the state police force. A three-judge federal district court sustained the constitutionality of the exclusion over the claim that it violated the equal protection clause of the Fourteenth Amendment.

101

Question: Does the equal protection clause shield aliens against wholesale exclusion from a state police force?

Decision: No. Opinion by Chief Justice Burger. Vote: 6–3, Blackmun concurring in the result, Marshall, Brennan, and Stevens dissenting.

Reasons: When states deny welfare or education benefits to aliens or sharply circumscribe their employment opportunities, *Graham* v. *Richardson,* 403 U.S. 365 (1971), and its progeny require condemnation of the discrimination under the equal protection clause unless it is justified by a substantial government interest. Only a rational basis is needed, however, to justify a state's exclusion of aliens from voting or the occupancy of public offices involving "discretionary decision-making, or execution of policy, which substantially affects members of the political community." This relaxed level of equal protection scrutiny simply reflects the fact that in a democratic society the right to govern is reserved to citizens.

Although police officers do not formulate policy, they are clothed with a wide variety of discretionary powers: to search dwellings without a warrant, to stop and frisk persons in public places, and to make warrantless arrests. The abuse of these powers may seriously injure individuals, and their proper exercise fulfills a fundamental obligation of government to its constituency. Police officers are thus direct participants in the execution of broad public policy.

> [M]ost States expressly confine the employment of police officers to citizens, whom the State may reasonably presume to be more familiar with and sympathetic to American traditions. . . . In the enforcement and execution of the laws the police function is one where citizenship bears a rational relationship to the special demands of the particular position.

Domestic Relations

Under the doctrines of due process and equal protection, the Court examined three aspects of domestic relations this term. In *Zablocki* v. *Redhail,* 434 U.S. 374 (1978), a statutory barrier to marriage that confronted only persons having an obligation to support their natural children in the custody of others was overturned under the equal protection clause. The statute in question permitted such persons to marry only upon proof of compliance with their support obligations and a likelihood that their children would not become public charges.

This heavy burden on the freedom to marry, the Court observed, was unnecessary to safeguard the economic welfare of out-of-custody children because assignment of wages, civil contempt proceedings, and criminal penalties were available to exact compliance with support obligations.

An unwed father's quest to control adoption of his natural child was the source of dispute in *Quilloin* v. *Walcott,* 434 U.S. 246 (1978). Under state law, the father was denied an absolute veto over the adoption of his illegitimate child, an authority that was offered to married, divorced, or separated fathers with respect to their children. Noting that the unwed father could obtain veto authority either by marrying the mother or legitimating the child by court order, a unanimous Court found no due process or equal protection vice in his unfavorable treatment under the contested adoption law.

A dispute over child support in a California state court brought forth a constitutional confrontation in *Kulko* v. *Superior Court,* 436 U.S. 84 (1978). A married couple, longtime residents of New York who had two small children, obtained a divorce, the terms of which obliged the father to pay child support during school vacations, when the children would reside with the mother in California, her newly acquired domicile. The children were to reside with the father in New York during the school year. Subsequently, at the request of the children, the father permitted them to travel to California and to reside permanently with the mother. The mother then sued the father in California state court seeking to increase his support obligations. The father interposed a due process objection to the state court's exercise of personal jurisdiction over him because his purposeful contacts with California were so much attenuated. By a 6–3 vote, the Supreme Court upheld the due process defense. It noted, however, that due process would not prevent the mother from invoking uniform reciprocal enforcement of support laws that empowered her to file a child-support petition in a California court and have its merits determined by a New York court without traveling there.

Zablocki v. *Redhail,* 434 U.S. 374 (1978)

Facts: A Wisconsin statute prohibits a certain class of residents of Wisconsin from marrying within the state or elsewhere unless a court order granting permission to marry is obtained. The class includes persons lacking custody of their minor children but obliged to support them by judicial decree. A court may not authorize a member of this class to marry unless proof of compliance with his support obligations and a showing that the children covered by the support order are neither public charges nor likely to become so are forthcoming. Lacking the necessary proof for an order granting permission to marry, the father of an illegitimate child brought suit, attacking the constitutionality of the statute under the equal protection clause of the Fourteenth Amendment. A three-judge federal district court sustained the equal protection attack.

Question: Does the equal protection clause condemn Wisconsin's statutory interference with the right to marry?

Decision: Yes. Opinion by Justice Marshall. Vote: 8–1, Stewart, Powell, and Stevens concurring in the judgment, Rehnquist dissenting.

Reasons: The right to marry is a fundamental liberty protected by the due process clause of the Fourteenth Amendment. Statutory classifications that "significantly interfere" with this right survive equal protection scrutiny only if they are supported by, and closely tailored to effectuate, important state interests. The questioned Wisconsin statute interferes "directly and substantially" with the right of members of the affected class to marry. They must obtain a court order, which will be denied if they either lack the financial means to satisfy their support obligations or cannot prove that their children will not become public charges. Even applicants for marriage who are capable of obtaining the permission of the court, moreover, suffer a serious intrusion into their exercise of a fundamental freedom. Accordingly, the Wisconsin statute must undergo strict equal protection review.

Wisconsin proffers two legitimate and substantial state interests as justification for its statute: counseling marriage applicants as to the necessity of fulfilling their prior support obligations and protecting the welfare of their out-of-custody children. The first interest, however, is not advanced by denying permission to marry once counseling has been completed, and the questioned statute is unnecessary to effectuation of the second goal. The state possesses several alternatives for exacting compliance with support obligations: assignments of wages, civil contempt proceedings, and criminal penalties. In addition, out-of-custody children may be prevented from becoming public charges by adjusting the level of payments required by support orders. Finally, the statute tramples too carelessly on the right to marry to be sustained as a vehicle for forestalling defaults in meeting existing support obligations by preventing the incurring of new support obligations through marriage. Wisconsin does not prohibit other financial commitments that may jeopardize support obligations, and the contested statute may prevent marriage that could enhance an applicant's ability to satisfy these obligations. The statute is insufficiently tailored to the protection of out-of-custody children to survive exacting scrutiny under the equal protection clause. This conclusion, however, does not "suggest that every state regulation which relates in any way to the incidents of or prerequisites for marriage must be subjected to rigorous scrutiny."

Quilloin v. *Walcott,* 434 U.S. 246 (1978)

Facts: Under Georgia law the consent of both parents is generally made a condition of the adoption of a child born in wedlock. In contrast, only the consent of the mother is required for the adoption of an illegitimate child. The father of an illegitimate child may acquire such veto authority by legitimating his offspring, either by marrying the mother and acknowledging the child as his own, or by obtaining a court order declaring the child legitimate and capable of inheriting from him.

A natural father, having failed to legitimate his child, sought to block adoption of the child by the natural mother and her husband. After receiving testimony from the father, the prospective adoptive parents, and other witnesses, a state court found that the proposed adoption was in the best interests of the child and thus granted the adoption petition. The natural father argued unsuccessfully to the Georgia Supreme Court that the due process and equal protection clauses of the Fourteenth Amendment required that he be given veto authority over adoption of his child absent a finding of his unfitness as a parent.

Question: Did application of the Georgia adoption laws to deny the unwed father authority to prevent adoption of his illegitimate child violate either the due process or equal protection clauses?

Decision: No. Opinion by Justice Marshall for a unanimous Court.

Reasons: The due process clause protects several aspects of family life and parent-child relationships. In this case, however, denying the unwed father authority to block the adoption of his child did not offend these constitutionally protected values. The father had never sought custody of his child, and the adoption enhanced an existing family unit, a result desired by all except the father. "Whatever might be required in other situations, we cannot say that the State was required in this situation to find anything more than that the adoption . . . was in the 'best interests of the child.' "

The equal protection argument is also flawed. It is founded on the assertion that unwed fathers are entitled to the identical veto authority that married, divorced, or separated fathers possess over adoption of their children. But unlike the unwed father in this case, the latter class of fathers has at some time shouldered significant responsibilities with respect to the daily supervision, education, protection, or care of their children. "Under any standard of review, the State was not foreclosed from recognizing this difference in the extent of commitment to the welfare of the child."

Kulko v. *Superior Court of California,* 436 U.S. 84 (1978)

Facts: Ezra Kulko and his wife, longtime domiciliaries and residents of New York, executed a separation agreement in New York City in 1972 that provided, *inter alia,* that their two children would stay with their father during the school year but would spend vacations with their mother, who had recently moved to California. In addition, Mr. Kulko agreed to pay his wife $3,000 annually in child support for the period when the children were in her custody. Subsequently, Mrs. Kulko procured a divorce decree in Haiti that incorporated the terms of the separation agreement. In 1973, one child voiced a desire to live with her mother and spend vacations with her father. Mr. Kulko agreed to this alteration in living arrangements and purchased a plane ticket to California for the child. In 1976, the other child requested an identical change in custody arrangements, and he used a plane ticket secretly provided by the mother to fly to California. Shortly thereafter, the mother sued Mr. Kulko in California state court, seeking to increase his child-support obligations. Kulko moved to quash service of the complaint on the ground that his contacts with California were constitutionally insufficient to warrant the state's assertion of personal jurisdiction over him. The trial court's denial of the motion was affirmed by the California Supreme Court. It reasoned that Mr. Kulko had purposely availed himself of the benefits and protection of California laws by sending his daughter there; and although his son flew to California without his aid, it was nevertheless fair and reasonable to exert personal jurisdiction over him with respect to both children since he had consented to their permanent residence in California. Accordingly, the California Supreme Court ruled that due process did not shield Mr. Kulko from the state court's exercise of personal jurisdiction for purposes of adjudicating the child support dispute.

Question: Were Mr. Kulko's contacts with California sufficient to provide a constitutional foundation for the exercise of personal jurisdiction over him by its state courts to adjudicate the child support dispute?

Decision: No. Opinion by Justice Marshall. Vote: 6–3, Brennan, White, and Powell dissenting.

Reasons: The due process clause of the Fourteenth Amendment circumscribes the power of state courts to adjudicate disputes affecting rights or interests of nonresident defendants. Due process shields a defendant against state jurisdiction except where he has had sufficient purposeful contact with the state to make it "reasonable" and "fair" to require the litigation of his defenses there.

In this case, the exercise of state jurisdiction was founded on Mr. Kulko's acquiescence in his daughter's desire to live in California with her mother. This arrangement, however, taken to promote family harmony, was not the offspring of purposeful action by Mr. Kulko taken to avail himself of the benefits and protection of California laws. The arrangement modified a separation agreement negotiated in New York, moreover, and was not undertaken to advance Mr. Kulko's commercial interests. Finally, Mr. Kulko could not reasonably anticipate that his single act of permitting his daughter to reside in California would justify the substantial financial burden and personal strain of litigating a child-support suit in a forum 3,000 miles away. To uphold jurisdiction in this type of case would aggravate family relations. Mr. Kulko had insufficient purposeful contacts with California to justify the assertion of personal jurisdiction over him by its state courts.

This conclusion does not denigrate California's interests in protecting the welfare of minor residents and cultivating healthy family environments. Both California and New York have adopted uniform reciprocal enforcement of support laws that would permit the divorced wife to file her child support petition in a California court and have its merits determined by a New York court without her traveling there. It is also noteworthy that California has voiced no exceptional interest in adjudicating child support cases by enacting a special jurisdictional statute for such disputes or otherwise.

Labor Law

The 1977–1978 term yielded important victories in litigation for both management and labor in battles concerning union organizing, picketing, and influence over the political process. Efforts by labor to urge legislation advantageous to union workers through newsletters were endorsed in *Eastex Inc.* v. *NLRB,* 437 U.S. 556 (1978). At issue was whether an employer had committed an unfair labor practice by prohibiting the distribution of a union newsletter on his property that urged employees to oppose a right-to-work proposal, criticized President Nixon's veto of minimum-wage legislation, and advocated electoral support for candidates sympathetic to labor. The National Labor Relations Act, the Court declared, protects collective activity of employees that is aimed at maintaining or improving working conditions through the political process. If the distribution of union newsletters in furtherance of such political action avoids prejudice to interests of management, the Court explained, then the National Labor Relations Board may prohibit the employer from suppressing the distribution on his property.

Union organizing activities in hospitals were given a boost in *Beth Israel Hospital* v. *NLRB,* 437 U.S. 483 (1978). There the Court upheld the NLRB's condemnation of a hospital rule that prohibited employees from soliciting union support or distributing union literature during nonworking time in the hospital cafeteria and coffee shop. Absent special circumstances, the Court concluded, an employer may not restrict solicitation of employees by a union during nonworking time in nonworking areas.

Management will enjoy wider opportunities to enjoin trespassory union picketing in the wake of *Sears, Roebuck & Co.* v. *San Diego County District Council of Carpenters,* 436 U.S. 180 (1978). The question raised in that case was whether a state court was pre-empted from entertaining a trespass action seeking to enjoin union picketing because of potential conflicts with overriding federal labor policies. The Court expounded the purpose and scope of the pre-emption doctrine in *San Diego Building Trades Council* v. *Garmon,* 359 U.S. 236 (1959): "When an activity is arguably subject to the [protection of section 7 of the National Labor Relations Act or the prohibition of section 8], the states as well as federal courts must defer to the exclusive competence of the National Labor Relations Board if the danger of state interference with national policy is to be averted." The decision in *Sears, Roebuck* cut back on the pre-emption doctrine by sustaining state jurisdiction over Sears's trespass claim against union picketing. Where the state interest at stake is compelling and the threatened disruption of national labor policy is insubstantial, said the Court, then state courts may entertain challenges to union activity.

A quest by management to secure aid in preparing a defense against a charge of unfair labor practice by invoking the Freedom of

Information Act was rebuffed in *NLRB* v. *Robbins Tire and Rubber Co.*, 437 U.S. 214 (1978). The Court held that the NLRB could withhold statements of witnesses it intended to call at the hearing on the unfair labor practice without particularized proof that disclosure would actually interfere with the proceedings.

Eastex, Inc. v. *National Labor Relations Board*, 437 U.S. 556 (1978)

Facts: Section 7 of the National Labor Relations Act prohibits employers from interfering with concerted activity of employees "for the purpose of . . . mutual aid or protection." The National Labor Relations Board ruled that section 7 was offended by an employer's refusal to allow distribution of a union newsletter in nonworking areas of his property during nonworking time. One section of the newsletter urged employees to oppose a state constitutional proposal that would prohibit union or agency shops. Another section urged political opposition to then President Nixon for his veto of a minimum-wage law.

The court of appeals affirmed. It reasoned that section 7 protects the distribution of newsletters that are reasonably related to the jobs or plant status of employees and that do not disrupt the employer's business.

Question: Did section 7 protect distribution of the contested union newsletter in nonworking areas of the employer's property during nonworking time?

Decision: Yes. Opinion by Justice Powell. Vote: 7–2, Rehnquist and Burger dissenting.

Reasons: Section 7 offers protection to concerted activity by employees whether or not it is inspired by a dispute with their employer or in furtherance of employment-related goals that can be attained only through the political process. Minimum-wage and right-to-work laws have a powerful influence on wages and union power. Accordingly, the distribution of literature urging employees to influence the political process on such issues falls within the protective ambit of section 7.

This protection is not lost simply because the distribution occurs on the property of an employer. Where, as here, there is no showing that management interests would be prejudiced by the distribution, the property rights of the employer may be subordinated to the interests of employees in seeking to bolster their collective-bargaining position.

Beth Israel Hospital v. National Labor Relations Board, 437 U.S. 483 (1978)

Facts: A nonprofit hospital adopted a rule prohibiting its employees from soliciting union support or distributing union literature during nonworking time in the hospital cafeteria and coffee shop. After a hearing, the National Labor Relations Board condemned the rule as an unlawful interference with employee rights of concerted activity protected by section 7 of the National Labor Relations Act. The board noted that approximately 77 percent of the cafeteria's patrons were employees while only 9 percent were visitors and 1.56 percent patients. It found that employees lacked access to alternative locations that could be used effectively to promote union goals, and that the hospital failed to demonstrate that its rule was necessary to safeguard patient care. The board thus concluded that solicitude for patient care could not justify the rule's curtailment of union activity. The court of appeals affirmed.

Question: Did the board err in overturning the contested rule prohibiting union activity in the hospital cafeteria and coffee shop?

Decision: No. Opinion by Justice Brennan. Vote: 9–0. Blackmun, Powell, Burger, and Rehnquist concurred in the judgment.

Reasons: In *Republic Aviation Corp.* v. *NLRB*, 324 U.S. 793 (1945), the Court endorsed the board's view that absent special circumstances, restrictions on employee solicitation during nonworking time and in nonworking areas offends section 7 of the National Labor Relations Act. Congress did not disturb this understanding of section 7 when nonprofit hospitals were brought within its embrace in 1974.

In this case, the board's conclusion that the contested rule was not founded on special circumstances was permissible. There was no showing that the rule was related to securing a tranquil environment for patient care, or that alternative locations for effective exercise of organizational rights were available to employees outside the cafeteria or coffee shop. The rule, therefore, ran afoul of the board's permissible interpretation of section 7 rights as applied to health-care facilities; it denied employee solicitation and distribution activity during nonworking time in nonworking areas and was unnecessary to forestall disruption of health care operations or disturbance of patients.

Sears, Roebuck and Co. v. San Diego County District Council of Carpenters, 436 U.S. 180 (1978)

Facts: Confronted with peaceful union picketers on its privately owned walkways, Sears, Roebuck and Co. obtained an injunction from the California Superior Court against the continuing trespass. The California Supreme Court reversed. Observing that the picketing was intended to secure work for union members and to publicize the undercutting by Sears of prevailing benefit levels for the employment of carpenters, the court concluded that section 7 of the National Labor Relations Act (NLRA) offered arguable protection for the trespass. On the other hand, the court stated, the trespass was also arguably prohibited under section 8(b)(7)(c) of the act as unlawful recognitional picketing. Because the contested activity was arguably governed by sections 7 and 8 of the act, the court held that state jurisdiction over the trespass was pre-empted by the National Labor Relations Board under the guidelines announced in *San Diego Building Trades* v. *Garmon,* 359 U.S. 236 (1959).

Question: Did the California state courts lack jurisdiction over the picketing dispute because the trespass in question was arguably subject to sections 7 and 8 of the National Labor Relations Act?

Decision: No. Opinion by Justice Stevens. Vote 6–3, Brennan, Stewart, and Marshall dissenting.

Reasons: As a matter of California state law, the union picketing was condemned solely because of its location; its objectives were beyond reproach under state law. As a matter of federal law, the legality of the picketing under sections 7 and 8 of the NLRA would be controlled largely by its objectives. These considerations are critical to the application of the prophylactic guidelines announced in *Garmon:*

> When an activity is arguably subject to section 7 or section 8 of the Act, the States as well as the federal courts must defer to the exclusive competence of the National Labor Relations Board if the danger of state interference with national policy is to be averted.

When picketing is arguably prohibited as a matter of federal law, judicial deference to the NLRB is generally necessary to secure uniform application of substantive law and to forestall conflicting remedies. The assertion of state jurisdiction over the picketing dispute in this case, however, did not jeopardize these federal interests. A determination by the NLRB of whether the picketing was prohibited under federal law would turn on an examination of its objectives. In contrast, Sears's trespass claim questioned only the location of the picketing. Resolution of the claim by the state court, therefore, threatened no inconsistency or interference with any prospective assessment by the NLRB of the legality of the picketing under federal law. The reasons for pre-empting judicial resolution of union activity arguably prohibited under federal law, therefore, do not justify condemnation of the California courts for examining the trespassory aspects of union picketing at issue in this case.

The *Garmon* doctrine also prevents state judicial inquiry into union activity that is arguably protected by federal law. This rule is designed to forestall unconstitutional state interference with conduct that is sanctioned by the NLRA. Three factors, however, justify subordinating this concern and permitting state resolution of Sears's trespass claim. First, Sears was prevented as a matter of federal law from seeking a decision from the NLRB as to whether the picketing was protected activity. Second, most trespassory activity of unions is unprotected under federal law. Thus, there is little risk that state courts will enjoin a trespass that the labor board would have protected. Finally, a union confronted with a demand to cease trespassory picketing may file a charge of unfair labor practice with the board to resolve the issue of protection.

> Because the assertion of state jurisdiction in a case of this kind does not create a significant risk of prohibition of protected conduct, we are unwilling to presume that Congress intended the arguably protected character of the Union's conduct to deprive the California courts of jurisdiction to entertain Sears' trespass action.

National Labor Relations Board v. *Robbins Tire & Rubber Co.*, 437 U.S. 214 (1978)

Facts: The Freedom of Information Act (FOIA), 5 U.S. Code 552, establishes a broad policy of disclosure of government records, but contains nine exempt categories. Under exemption 7(A) of the FOIA, investigatory materials compiled for purposes of law enforcement may be withheld if their production would "interfere with enforcement proceedings." Relying on this exemption, the National Labor Relations Board (NLRB) refused to disclose, prior to its hearing on an unfair labor practice complaint, statements of witnesses it intended to call. A federal district court held that exemption 7(A) failed to shelter the statements of these witnesses because there was no specific evidentiary showing by the board that their prehearing disclosure would engender intimidation of the witnesses or otherwise actually interfere with the enforcement proceeding. The court of appeals affirmed.

Question: Did exemption 7(A) shield the statements of prospective witnesses for the NLRB from prehearing production despite the absence of proof that disclosure would actually interfere with the board's pending enforcement proceeding?

Decision: Yes. Opinion by Justice Marshall. Vote: 7–2, Powell and Brennan dissenting in part.

Reasons: The language and legislative history of exemption 7(A) reveal an intent to permit generic determinations that disclosure of particular types of investigatory records would generally interfere with enforcement proceedings. The NLRB determined properly that prehearing disclosure of statements of prospective witnesses would generally obstruct fair resolution of pending charges of unfair labor practices. If withholding were permitted only on a particular showing of interference, litigation would be spawned to the detriment of speedy resolution of such charges. History teaches, moreover, that intimidation of witnesses is endemic to labor-management disputes, although it is seldom susceptible to evidentiary proof. Finally, prehearing withholding of statements of witnesses does not offend the guiding vision of the FOIA: to create an informed citizenry, to check corruption, and to hold public officials accountable to the people.

Federal Courts and Procedure

Class-action plaintiffs were dealt a trilogy of procedural setbacks this term, adding to similar defeats suffered in recent years.[13] In *Coopers & Lybrand* v. *Livesay*, 437 U.S. 463 (1978), a unanimous Court held that a district court order refusing to certify a putative class was not a final decision eligible for immediate review under 28 U.S. Code

---

[13] See Eisen v. Carlisle & Jacquelin, 417 U.S. 156 (1974), holding that Rule 23(b)(3) of the Federal Rules of Civil Procedure requires class-action representatives to shoulder the costs of sending individual notice to all class members who can be identified with reasonable effort; Zahn v. International Paper Company, 414 U.S. 291 (1973), holding that all class members must suffer injury in excess of $10,000 to satisfy the jurisdictional requirements of 28 U.S. Code 1332(a).

113

1291. Although such an order might sound the death knell of the suit when the representative plaintiffs lacked the resources necessary to litigate their individual claims, the Court declared, this fact offered no justification for modifying the statutory standards of finality. A related issue was raised in *Gardner* v. *Westinghouse Broadcasting Co.*, 437 U.S. 478 (1978). In that case a class plaintiff sought to obtain interlocutory review under 28 U.S. Code 1292(a)(1) of a denial of class certification. That section permits review of interlocutory orders that are refusals of injunctive relief. Since the order denying class-action status circumscribed the scope of potential injunctive relief, the plaintiff urged, it was tantamount to refusing to grant an injunction. The Court unanimously rejected that argument.

The unmistakable teaching of *Oppenheimer Fund, Inc.* v. *Sanders*, 437 U.S. 340 (1978), coupled with the complementary ruling in *Eisen* v. *Carlisle & Jacquelin*, 417 U.S. 156 (1974), is that class-action plaintiffs proceeding under Rule 23(b)(3) of the Federal Rules of Civil Procedure will ordinarily be required to bear all the costs of identifying the members of the class and sending notice of the pendency of the action. *Eisen* held that a plaintiff representing a class must ordinarily pay the costs of notifying all members of that class whose identity can be obtained through reasonable efforts. The question confronted in *Oppenheimer* was whether a district court could order a defendant to bear the cost of identifying class members under Rule 23. The Court answered that it could, but only under special circumstances. If the costs of identification were substantial when measured in absolute dollars, the Court explained, then they must be reimbursed by the plaintiff. The Court concluded that $16,000 in expenses incurred by defendants in identifying class members in *Oppenheimer* was substantial and thus must be paid by plaintiffs.

Federal district courts have original jurisdiction over suits between citizens of different states that arise under state law when the amount in controversy exceeds $10,000.[14] These so-called diversity suits at present represent approximately 25 percent of all civil litigation in federal district courts.[15] The heavy caseloads of federal courts,[16] their relative inexperience with issues at state law, and a diminishing likelihood of prejudice on the part of state courts against

---

[14] 28 U.S. Code 1332(a).

[15] *Annual Report of the Director*, Administrative Office of U.S. Courts, p. 5, Table 6 (1978).

[16] In fiscal 1978, 18,918 cases were filed in the federal courts of appeals, an increase of 107.5 percent since 1968. Ibid., p. 3, Table 5. During the same period, 166,539 cases were filed in federal district courts, or 417 cases per authorized judgeship. Ibid., p. 57. To help relieve this burden, the 95th Congress passed legislation creating 35 additional federal appellate judgeships and 117 additional district court judgeships. Act of Oct. 20, 1978, P.L. 95–486, 92 Stat. 1629 (1978).

noncitizens has spurred legislative attempts to eliminate most federal diversity jurisdiction.[17] The decision in *Owen Equipment and Erection Co. v. Kroger*, 437 U.S. 365 (1978), was consonant with this legislative movement. It interpreted section 1332 narrowly to deny federal ancillary jurisdiction over a claim asserted by the plaintiff against a third-party defendant who is a resident of the same state.

In *Elkins* v. *Moreno*, 435 U.S. 647 (1978), federal courts were instructed to defer to state adjudication of issues at state law if constitutional questions might thereby be avoided. The Court also curtailed the mandamus powers of federal appellate courts in *Will* v. *Calvert Fire Insurance Co.*, 437 U.S. 655 (1978), by concluding that matters committed to a district court's discretion, such as the setting of its own calendar, may not be overturned by writs of mandamus.

Coopers & Lybrand v. Livesay, 437 U.S. 463 (1978)

Facts: Buyers of Punte Gorda Isles securities filed suit on behalf of themselves and a class of similarly situated purchasers, alleging violations of several federal laws concerning securities. The district court ruled that the suit could not be maintained as a class action under Rule 23 of the Federal Rules of Civil Procedure. Plaintiffs sought immediate appellate review of that order under 28 U.S. Code 1291. The court of appeals concluded that the order sounded the death knell of the action because the limited resources of plaintiffs would, as a practical matter, foreclose pursuit of their individual claims. Accordingly, it held that section 1291 conferred jurisdiction to entertain the appeal and reversed the district court order.

Question: Is a district court's ruling that an action may not be maintained as a class action under Rule 23 subject to appellate review under 28 U.S. Code 1291?

Decision: No. Opinion by Justice Stevens for a unanimous Court.

Reasons: Courts of appeals may entertain appeals under section 1291 only from final decisions of district courts. Generally speaking, a final decision is one that ends the litigation on the merits. A refusal to certify a class, however, does not terminate the litigation because

---

[17] The House of Representatives passed legislation in which federal diversity jurisdiction was virtually abolished by a vote of 266 to 133 during the 95th Congress. *Congressional Record* H1553, H1569–70 daily ed. (February 28, 1978). The Senate refused to agree to such a drastic curtailment of diversity jurisdiction, thereby causing the pending legislation to die.

a representative plaintiff may nevertheless pursue his individual claim.

In addition, such rulings are not embraced by the narrow "collateral order" exception to the final judgment rule of section 1291 fashioned in *Cohen* v. *Beneficial Industrial Loan Corp.*, 337 U.S. 541 (1949). *Cohen* excepts only orders that conclusively determine an important disputed issue entirely apart from the merits of the suit and that could not be reviewed on appeal from a final judgment. Class-action rulings, in contrast, may be revised under Rule 23(e)(1), are ordinarily enmeshed with factual and legal issues going to the merits of the suit, and are subject to effective review after final judgment.

To add a death-knell exception to section 1291 whenever interlocutory orders would, as a practical matter, terminate the litigation adversely to plaintiffs prior to final judgment, would be to contradict the fundamental policy against piecemeal review of a single controversy expressed in the section. It would delay the administration of justice by requiring a detailed inquiry into the resources of plaintiffs and their subjective commitment to pursuing their individual claims. Congress enacted the Interlocutory Appeals Act, 28 U.S. Code 1292(b), to permit prompt review, with the consent of the trial judge and the appellate court, of nonfinal orders that turn on the facts of a particular case. The death-knell doctrine would circumvent this statute by authorizing indiscriminate interlocutory review of orders given by trial judges. Allowing appeals of such nonfinal orders as a matter of right, moreover, would thrust appellate courts into the trial process, thus defeating a vital purpose of the final-judgment rule, that of maintaining the appropriate relationships between the respective courts.

Gardner v. *Westinghouse Broadcasting Co.*, 437 U.S. 478 (1978)

Facts: Seeking injunctive relief against unlawful sex discrimination, a woman moved to maintain a class-action suit against a broadcaster under Rule 23(b) of the Federal Rules of Civil Procedure. The district court denied the motion, and the court of appeals refused to entertain an appeal of the denial under 28 U.S. Code 1292(a)(1). That provision authorizes appellate review of interlocutory orders refusing injunctions. Because broader injunctive relief in the litigation would have been available to a class rather than to an individual, the plaintiff urged that the denial of class certification was tantamount to refusing a substantial portion of injunctive relief.

Question: Does section 1292(a)(1) authorize review of class-action rulings that indirectly circumscribe the scope of potential injunctive relief?

Decision: No. Opinion by Justice Stevens for a unanimous Court.

Reasons: Section 1292(a)(1) creates a narrow exception to the long-established congressional policy against piecemeal appeals. It is available only to litigants confronted with interlocutory orders the effects of which would be irreparable. Orders denying class certification, in contrast, may be revised and do not affect the merits of individual claims for injunctive relief. Accordingly, a refusal to certify a class in a suit in which injunctive relief is sought cannot be appealed under section 1292(a)(1).

Oppenheimer Fund, Inc. v. *Sanders,* **437 U.S. 340 (1978)**

Facts: Representative plaintiffs in a class action brought under Rule 23(b)(3) of the Federal Rules of Civil Procedure must bear the costs of providing individual notice to all members of the class who can be identified through reasonable effort. In a class action brought by shareholders of a mutual fund in which securities fraud by the fund's directors, officers, and managers was alleged, a district court ordered the defendants to compile from their records a list of all members of the class. The mutual fund's transfer agent could develop the list by sorting manually through voluminous paper records, key-punching hundreds of thousands of computer cards, and creating eight new computer programs, all at a cost of approximately $16,000. Plaintiffs were responsible under the order for preparing the necessary notice and mailing it at their expense.

Affirming the order, the court of appeals rejected the contentions that the district court lacked power either to order class-action defendants to assist in identifying class members or to bear the costs of such a task.

Questions: (1) Does Rule 23 empower federal district courts to compel defendants in a class action to assist in identifying members of the class and to bear the costs of identification in some limited circumstances? (2) Did the district court abuse its discretion in requiring defendants to shoulder the $16,000 burden of identifying class members in this case?

Decision: Yes to both questions. Opinion by Justice Powell for a unanimous Court.

Reasons: Rule 23(d) clearly vests power in the district court to order either the representative plaintiffs of a class or the defendants to perform the tasks necessary to send notice to all members of the class. Plaintiffs must ordinarily shoulder this burden to remain faithful to the general principle that parties must finance their suits. A defendant capable of performing a necessary task with less difficulty or at lesser expense than the representative plaintiff, however, may be required to do so by the district court. In such cases, the representative plaintiff must pay the costs of the defendant's performance if it is substantial. The test of substantiality should be applied with reference to the principle underlying *Eisen* v. *Carlisle & Jacquelin,* 417 U.S. 156 (1974) "that the representative plaintiff should bear all costs relating to the sending of notice because it is he who seeks to maintain the suit as a class action."

In this case, the district court abused its discretion in requiring defendants to bear the $16,000 cost of identifying class members. The expense of hiring the mutual fund's transfer agent to prepare the necessary list would be identical for either plaintiffs or defendants; it should thus have remained with the plaintiffs, since no special circumstances justified an opposite result. Neither the comparative wealth of a defendant nor an allegation of wrongdoing is a fair reason for requiring a defendant to subsidize a plaintiff's case.

Owen Equipment and Erection Co. v. *Kroger,* 437 U.S. 365 (1978)

Facts: Invoking the diversity jurisdiction of federal courts under 28 U.S. Code 1332, a resident of Iowa filed a wrongful-death action against a Nebraska corporation. The latter filed a third-party complaint against an Iowa corporation under Rule 14(a) of the Federal Rules of Civil Procedure in which the Nebraska corporation alleged that negligence on the part of the Iowa corporation had caused the death underlying the plaintiff's complaint. The Iowa plaintiff then amended her complaint to include the Iowa corporation as a defendant. The Iowa corporation moved to dismiss the complaint as to itself on the ground that diversity jurisdiction under section 1332 was lacking. The district court denied the motion and the court of appeals affirmed.

Question: Does section 1332 confer jurisdiction on federal district courts to entertain a claim asserted by a plaintiff against a third-party defendant of the same state?

Decision: No. Opinion by Justice Stewart. Vote: 7–2, White and Brennan dissenting.

Reasons: In *United Mine Workers* v. *Gibbs*, 383 U.S. 715 (1966), the Court concluded that the federal judicial power could constitutionally embrace a pendent jurisdiction over state claims if two conditions were satisfied. First, the state and federal claims must be derived from a "common nucleus of operative fact." Second, the plaintiff would ordinarily be expected to try both claims in one proceeding. In this case, it may be assumed that the exercise of ancillary jurisdiction by the district court over the nondiverse claim asserted by the plaintiff against the third-party defendant was not constitutionally barred. That claim and the diversity claim stemmed from a common nucleus of fact.

Section 1332, however, is not coextensive with the maximum constitutional jurisdiction of district courts. It requires that all plaintiffs and defendants be citizens of different states. This requirement would be flouted by permitting jurisdiction over nondiverse third-party defendants; plaintiffs would simply sue diverse defendants and wait for them to implead nondiverse parties. Ancillary jurisdiction under section 1332 has been sustained when it has been necessary to protect claims that would otherwise be forfeited or that are inextricably entwined with the primary suit. Claims asserted by defendants involuntarily haled into court may also be reached by ancillary jurisdiction. These practical needs, however, offer no foundation for extending "the doctrine of ancillary jurisdiction to a plaintiff's cause of action against a citizen of the same State in a diversity case."

Elkins v. *Moreno*, 435 U.S. 647 (1978)

Facts: The University of Maryland adopted a general policy for deciding whether a student would be granted status as a resident for determination of admission, tuition, and charge differentials. It offers preferred status only to students who are either domiciled in Maryland or are financially dependent on parents domiciled there. Additionally, the university may deny resident status to those who do not pay the full spectrum of Maryland taxes. Invoking this policy, the university denied resident status for determining tuition to nonimmigrant alien students who were dependent on parents residing in Maryland but who held "G–4 visas"—nonimmigrant visas issued to officers or employees of international treaty organizations and members of their immediate families. The denial was founded on the belief that persons possessing G–4 visas are incapable of domiciliary status in Maryland because they are legally prevented from possessing the requisite intent to live there permanently or indefinitely. The nonimmigrant students attacked the denial in federal district court under

119

the due process and equal protection clauses of the Fourteenth Amendment and the Immigration and Nationality Act of 1952. Concluding that G–4 aliens possess the legal capacity to change domicile as a matter of federal law, the district court held that due process prohibited the University from irrebuttably presuming that they lack a Maryland domicile. The court of appeals affirmed.

Question: Should the district court have certified the case to the highest state court in Maryland for an authoritative decision on whether G–4 aliens are prevented from acquiring a Maryland domicile before reaching the constitutional questions raised by the nonimmigrant students?

Decision: Yes. Opinion by Justice Brennan. Vote: 7–2, Rehnquist and Burger dissenting.

Reasons: The Court has embraced a long-standing policy of avoiding unnecessary constitutional decisions. The dispute in this case may be resolved on nonconstitutional grounds if G–4 aliens have the capacity to acquire Maryland domiciles, a question without controlling precedents in Maryland common law. A Maryland statute authorizes the state court of appeals to answer questions of state law certified to it by the Supreme Court of the United States. Accordingly, the following question is certified to the Maryland Court of Appeals:

> Are persons residing in Maryland who hold or are named in a [G–4] visa . . . or who are financially dependent upon a person holding or named in such a visa, incapable as a matter of state law of becoming domiciliaries of Maryland?

In answering the question, the state court may be assisted in knowing that federal law neither requires G–4 aliens to maintain a permanent residence abroad nor requires that they pledge to leave the United States at a certain date. In addition, a G–4 alien who terminates his employment with an international treaty organization may ordinarily obtain the status of a permanent resident without leaving the United States.

Will v. *Calvert Fire Insurance Co.,* 437 U.S. 655 (1978)

Facts: Sued in state court for an alleged breach of an insurance contract, Calvert Fire Insurance defended on the grounds, *inter alia,* that violations of the Securities Act of 1933 and the Securities Exchange Act of 1934 rendered the agreement unenforceable. Calvert also filed affirmative claims for damages and equitable relief founded on these alleged violations in federal district court. To avoid duplicative litigation, the district court deferred ruling on all but one of the claims pending completion of the state suit; it permitted the damage claim under the 1934 act to proceed because the claim was subject to the exclusive jurisdiction of federal courts. The court of appeals granted a writ of mandamus directing the district court to proceed immediately to consider Calvert's 1934 Act claim for both damages and equitable relief.

Question: Did the court of appeals err in granting mandamus to overturn the exercise of the district court's discretion to control its own docket?

Decision: Yes. Plurality opinion by Justice Rehnquist. Vote: 5–4, Blackmun concurring in the judgment, Brennan, Burger, Powell, and Marshall dissenting.

Reasons: The All Writs Act, 28 U.S. Code 1651(a), sharply circumscribes the power of courts of appeals to issue writs of mandamus. The writ may be issued only when "necessary and appropriate in aid of their respective jurisdictions" and where the moving party has proven a "clear and indisputable" right to the writ.

In this case, the district court deferred consideration of all but Calvert's damage claim under the 1934 act because of the pendency of concurrent proceedings in state courts. Although the suit in state court was no bar to the exercise of federal jurisdiction, it was relevant to the district court's exercise of discretion to defer ruling on the federal claims.

> No one can seriously contend that a busy federal trial judge, confronted both with competing demands on his time for matters properly within his jurisdiction and with inevitable scheduling difficulties because of the unavailability of lawyers, parties, and witnesses, is not entrusted with a wide latitude in setting his own calendar.

The district court's decision to defer was tantamount to setting its own calendar and should not have been overridden by a writ of mandamus. Matters committed to a district court's discretion do not confer upon a litigant a clear and indisputable right to a particular result.

Federal Regulation of Business: Antitrust, Securities, Environmental, and Patent Law

The Court spoke as a champion of competition in a series of cases concerning the federal antitrust laws. In *National Society of Professional Engineers* v. *United States*, 435 U.S. 679 (1978), the Court ruled that anticompetitive practices cannot be exonerated under the Sherman Act simply because they further safety, health, or other policies, and anticompetitive restraints imposed by political subdivisions, the Court declared in *City of Lafayette* v. *Louisiana Power and Light Co.*, 435 U.S. 389 (1978), may be attacked under the Sherman Act unless they are directed or authorized by state law. In addition, foreign governments were granted authority to maintain treble damage actions for antitrust violations in *Pfizer, Inc.* v. *Government of India*, 434 U.S. 308 (1978).

While holding that intent is a necessary element of a crime under the Sherman Act, the Court refused, in *United States* v. *U.S. Gypsum Co.*, 438 U.S. 422 (1978), to recognize a claimed exemption from prohibitions of that act against unreasonable exchanges of price information. Specifically, it held that such exchanges are not removed from scrutiny under the Sherman Act even if undertaken to establish a defense against a possible charge of unlawful price discrimination under the Robinson-Patman Act.

Although stemming from a dispute having to do with international trade, the decision in *Zenith Radio Corporation* v. *United States*, 437 U.S. 443 (1978), carried significant implications with respect to competition for domestic industries threatened by waves of foreign imports. At issue was whether the remission of a Japanese value-added tax to Japanese exporters of electronic products constituted a bounty that required the United States to impose a countervailing duty on the products upon their importation. A unanimous Court held that the remission was not a bounty, thereby exposing American business to greater competition from foreign exporters.

The power of the Securities and Exchange Commission to police the trading of securities was curtailed in *SEC* v. *Sloan*, 436 U.S. 103 (1978). In that case, the Court rejected an interpretation of the Securities Exchange Act of 1934 that would have empowered the commission summarily to suspend trading in any security for an indefinite period.

Environmentalists were thwarted in their litigating endeavors to discourage or delay the development of nuclear power plants, but they were successful in challenging the opening of a hundred-million-dollar dam that would have threatened the habitat of the snail darter.

The Price-Anderson Act limits aggregate tort liability for a single nuclear accident to $560 million. An environmental group attacked the constitutionality of the ceiling on liability, urging that it encouraged irresponsibility in matters related to safety and the environment. The Court, however, found no constitutional vice in the legislative choice to encourage development of the nuclear power industry by limiting its exposure to liability in the event of a nuclear accident.[18] In *Vermont Yankee Nuclear Power Corporation* v. *Natural Resources Defense Council*, 435 U.S. 519 (1978), a federal court of appeals was sharply rebuked for shackling the Atomic Energy Commission (now the Nuclear Regulatory Commission) with procedural safeguards in its processing of applications for nuclear power licenses that were neither required by the Administrative Procedure Act nor the National Environmental Policy Act. Judicial review, the Court emphasized, provides no authority to overturn choices made by the political branches to develop nuclear energy.

The Endangered Species Act was invoked to enjoin the completion and opening of the Tellico Dam located on the Little Tennessee River in *Tennessee Valley Authority* v. *Hill*, 437 U.S. 153 (1978). The act commands all federal agencies to avoid jeopardizing the existence of an endangered species or destroying its critical habitat. The existence of the snail darter, an endangered species, would have been threatened by the operation of the Tellico Dam. A sharply divided Court held that neither successive appropriations measures nor equitable considerations permitted an interpretation of the act that would modify its sweeping and absolute protection of endangered species. The benefits of the Tellico Dam, the Court stated, must be subordinated to the continued existence of the snail darter. In the wake of this decision, Congress amended the Endangered Species Act to authorize the opening of the Tellico Dam and to permit other federal action that could threaten an endangered species, provided that an exemption is obtained from a seven-member committee.[19] An exemption may be granted only if the committee determines that there are no reasonable and prudent alternatives to the action of the agency, its benefits clearly outweigh those offered by alternative courses of action that would be consistent with conservation of the endangered species, and the action is of regional or national significance.

An attempt to bring a computer program within the protection of existing federal patent laws failed for a second time in *Parker* v.

---

[18] Duke Power Co. v. Carolina Environmental Study Group, Inc., 438 U.S. 59 (1978).
[19] Endangered Species Act Amendments of 1978, P.L. 95–632, 92 Stat. 3751 (1978).

Flook, 437 U.S. (1978).[20] The Court seemingly implored a contemporary Congress to address forthrightly the question of whether computer programs deserve patent protection in view of the importance of computers in modern business.

National Society of Professional Engineers v. *United States,* 435 U.S. 679 (1978)

Facts: The canons of ethics of the National Society of Professional Engineers prohibit competitive bidding. The prohibition was assailed by the United States in federal district court as a violation per se of the Sherman Act. Endorsing the government's claim, the district court ruled that the questioned canons could not be saved by proof that competitive bidding would engender inferior engineering work that would endanger the public safety. The court of appeals affirmed.

Question: Are anticompetitive practices sheltered from condemnation under the Sherman Act if they enhance safety or other values?

Decision: No. Opinion by Justice Stevens. Vote: 8–0, Blackmun and Rehnquist concurring in part and concurring in the judgment, Burger concurring in part and dissenting in part. Brennan did not participate.

Reasons: The Sherman Act frowns on all unreasonable restraints of trade. The reasonableness of any restraint is tested solely by its significance with respect to competition. If it merely regulates or promotes competition, it escapes taint; if it suppresses or destroys competition, it is vulnerable to attack under the Sherman Act.

The ban on competitive bidding in this case dampens price competition and substantially deprives customers of an opportunity to trade quality against price in purchasing engineering services. The society offered no offsetting competitive justification for the ban, relying instead on its alleged contribution to public safety. To accept this as a defense of anticompetitive restraints is tantamount to launching "a frontal assault on the basic policy of the Sherman Act." The premise of the defense is that the policy of the act to encourage competition may be subordinated to other public values in assessing the reasonableness of a restraint of trade. Well-settled antitrust jurisprudence offers no support for this novel proposition.

---

[20] In Gottshalk v. Benson, 409 U.S. 63 (1972), the Court denied patent protection to a method of programming a general-purpose digital computer to solve certain types of mathematical problems according to an algorithm.

The society also urges that the First Amendment condemns the district court order, as amended by the court of appeals, prohibiting its adoption of any official opinion or policy statement suggesting that competitive bidding is unethical. Freedom of speech, however, may be curtailed by injunctions narrowly tailored to dissipate the effects of an antitrust violation and to forestall a recurrence. The order challenged by the society went no further than was necessary to eliminate the evils caused by the society's illegal conduct.

City of Lafayette v. Louisiana Power and Light Co., 435 U.S. 389 (1978)

Facts: Cities in Louisiana are empowered under state law to own and operate utility systems both within and without their city limits. Two cities brought an action against an investor-owned utility, alleging that it had violated the Sherman Act. The private utility counterclaimed, alleging various antitrust violations, and the cities moved to dismiss the counterclaim on the ground that *Parker* v. *Brown*, 317 U.S. 338 (1943), shielded political subdivisions from federal antitrust attack. The district court granted the motion but the court of appeals reversed and remanded. It ruled that political subdivisions were clothed with antitrust immunity only with respect to activity authorized by the state legislature.

Question: Are anticompetitive restraints imposed by political subdivisions of states shielded from attack under the Sherman Act only when these restraints are authorized by state law?

Decision: Yes. Plurality opinion by Justice Brennan. Vote: 5–4, Burger concurring in the judgment and concurring in part, Stewart, White, Blackmun, and Rehnquist dissenting.

Reasons: Settled antitrust jurisprudence teaches that implied exemptions from the Sherman Act are disfavored because the act represents a transcendent national commitment to a regime of competition to spur American commerce. In *Parker* v. *Brown*, however, the Court recognized that deference to the concerns of federalism and state sovereignty justified an interpretation of the act that would exonerate states from liability for anticompetitive activities of the government. Municipalities, however, are entitled to a narrower immunity from the Sherman Act. Unlike states, they lack any constitutional claim of sovereignty. To offer approximately 60,000 different units of local government total freedom to pursue economic ends uncounseled by competitive principles, moreover, would introduce "a serious chink in the armor of antitrust protection."

> We . . . conclude that the *Parker* doctrine exempts only anticompetitive conduct engaged in as an act of government by the State as sovereign, or, by its subdivisions, pursuant to state policy to displace competition with regulation or monopoly public service.

The doctrine protects the anticompetitive activities of political subdivisions from challenge under the Sherman Act when it is found from authority conferred by the state that the state contemplated the type of action complained of. This will not impair the ability of states to delegate government power broadly to municipalities. "It means only that when the State itself has not directed or authorized an anticompetitive practice, the State's subdivisions in exercising their delegated powers must obey the antitrust laws."

Pfizer, Inc. v. *Government of India*, 434 U.S. 308 (1978)

Facts: Invoking section 4 of the Clayton Act, several foreign nations sued six pharmaceutical manufacturing companies in federal district court for alleged antitrust violations. Section 4 authorizes "[a]ny person" injured in his business or property by reason of an antitrust violation to maintain a suit for treble damages. The pharmaceutical companies moved to dismiss the suits on the theory that foreign nations are not "persons" entitled to sue for treble damages under section 4. The district court rejected that defense, and the court of appeals affirmed.

Question: Does section 4 of the Clayton Act authorize foreign nations to maintain treble-damage actions in federal courts?

Decision: Yes. Opinion by Justice Stewart. Vote: 5–3, Burger, Powell, and Rehnquist dissenting. Blackmun did not participate.

Reasons: Neither the express language nor legislative history of section 4 provides a clear answer to whether foreign nations were among its intended beneficiaries. The resolution of this issue must therefore be guided by an examination of the general policies underlying section 4.

Treble-damage actions advance two antitrust goals: deterrence of prospective violators and compensation of victims of antitrust violations. These purposes would be defeated by denying foreign nations authority to invoke the protection of section 4. The denial would permit antitrust violators to retain the fruits of their illegality at the expense of victimized foreign nations. In addition,

> [i]f foreign plaintiffs were not permitted to seek a remedy for their antitrust injuries, persons doing business both in this country and abroad might be tempted to enter into anticompetitive conspiracies affecting American consumers in the expectation that the illegal profits they could safely extort abroad would offset any liability to plaintiffs at home.

The dual policies of section 4 justify an interpretation that brings foreign nations within its remedial embrace. This conclusion is reinforced by *Georgia v. Evans*, 316 U.S. 159 (1942), in which the Court held that domestic states may invoke the treble-damage remedy of section 4. The Court explained that states possessed no other means of defense against antitrust violations and that the policies of section 4 would be thwarted by denying states a remedy offered to all other victims of antitrust violations. Foreign nations, like states, must generally seek relief against antitrust infractions through treble-damage suits, since criminal prosecutions or other remedies are unavailable. And congressional silence cannot justify excluding foreign nations from protection against treble damages, since it would affront the purposes of section 4. Accordingly, "a foreign nation, like a domestic state, is entitled to pursue the remedy of treble damages when it has been injured in its business or property by antitrust violations."

United States v. *U.S. Gypsum Co.,* 438 U.S. 422 (1978)

Facts: Several large manufacturers of gypsum board were indicted for conspiring to fix and stabilize prices in violation of section 1 of the Sherman Act. In furtherance of the conspiracy, the defendants were alleged to have exchanged information concerning current prices charged to specified customers. At trial, the defendants contended that these exchanges were undertaken in good faith to avoid violating the general proscription against price discrimination of the Robinson-Patman Act. This purpose, the defendants urged, would shelter the exchange from condemnation under the Sherman Act despite its stabilizing effect on prices. The district court disagreed and instructed the jury to return a verdict of guilty if it found that the effect of the exchange of information was to raise, fix, or maintain prices. Reversing on several grounds, the court of appeals held that under certain conditions exchanges of price information that stabilized prices would not offend the Sherman Act if they were inspired

127

solely by a desire to establish a defense to price discrimination under the Robinson-Patman Act.

Questions: (1) Did the district court err in instructing the jury to return a verdict of guilty without regard to the defendants' intent if the effect of the price information exchange was to stabilize prices? (2) Are exchanges of price information exempt from scrutiny under the Sherman Act if they are undertaken to establish a defense to a charge of price discrimination under the Robinson-Patman Act?

Decision: Yes to the first question and no to the second. Opinion by Chief Justice Burger. Votes: 6–2 and 7–1,respectively, Rehnquist and Stevens dissenting in part. Blackmun did not participate.

Reasons: Canons of statutory construction are based on a presumption that intent is an element of a criminal offense and counsel lenity in construing the ambit of ambiguous criminal statutes. As applied to the Sherman Act, these rules are especially compelling, because the act speaks in broad and general language. To hold competitors criminally accountable without regard to intent would deter salutary and procompetitive conduct lying close to the borderline of illegal terrain. Accordingly, intent is a necessary element of a criminal antitrust violation. An intent to fix prices through exchanges of information can be proved if the defendants had knowledge of its probable anticompetitive effects. Although a jury may infer intent from an effect on prices alone, it must remain free to accept or reject the inference.

The Robinson-Patman Act issue emerges from a defense offered by the act to its general prohibition against price discrimination among buyers. Section 2(b) of the act permits a seller to discriminate when it is necessary to meet an equally low price of a competitor. This defense is established if the seller's price concession was offered in good faith to match a competing offer. It does not require absolute certainty of a competitor's price. Interseller price verification, therefore, is ordinarily unnecessary to satisfy the good-faith standard of section 2(b). There may be a few situations in which verification is necessary to dispel doubts about the reliability of information concerning competing offers. The tendency for price discussions among oligopolists to stabilize prices and beget anticompetitive activity, however, requires that a seller either forgo a price concession or risk possible liability in such situations to advance the overriding policy of competition sponsored by the Sherman Act.

Zenith Radio Corporation v. *United States,* 437 U.S. 443 (1978)

Facts: Whenever a foreign country pays a bounty or grant upon the exportation of a product from its soil, the secretary of the treasury is required under 19 U.S. Code 1303(a) to levy a countervailing duty "equal to the net amount of such bounty or grant" upon importation of the product into the United States. Under Japanese law, manufacturers of electronic products are subject to a value-added tax that is based on a percentage of the sales price. If the products are exported, however, the taxes are remitted. Claiming that the remission constituted a bounty within the meaning of section 1303(a), Zenith Corporation filed suit in Customs Court seeking to compel the secretary of the treasury to levy a countervailing duty on the electronic products equal to the amount of the remission. The Customs Court granted the requested relief, but the Court of Customs and Patent Appeals reversed.

Question: Does the remission of the Japanese value-added tax upon the exportation of electronic products constitute a bounty within the meaning of section 1303(a)?

Decision: No. Opinion by Justice Marshall for a unanimous Court.

Reasons: The parent of section 1303(a) was section 5 of the Tariff Act of 1897. For more than eighty years and through five re-enactments of the statute, the secretary of the treasury has invariably construed the term *bounty* to exclude the remission of indirect taxes of the type challenged by Zenith. Congress has not acted to change this construction, which has also been incorporated into the General Agreement on Tariffs and Trade. Whether or not this construction should be changed because it may be unfair or is economically indefensible is a question for Congress, not the judiciary.

Isolated dicta in *Downs* v. *United States,* 187 U.S. 496 (1903), suggesting that any remission of a tax upon exports constitutes a bounty must be read in context and offer no justification for repudiating the secretary's interpretation in this case.

Securities and Exchange Commission v. *Sloan,* 436 U.S. 103 (1978)

Facts: The Securities and Exchange Commission (SEC) is empowered by section 12(k) of the Securities Exchange Act of 1934 "summarily to suspend trading in any security . . . for a period not exceeding ten days" if "in its opinion the public interest and the protection of investors so require." Invoking this authority, the commission issued a series of consecutive ten-day orders that foreclosed trading in the common stock of Canadian Javelin, Ltd. (CJL), for more than a year. The orders were founded on a single alleged manipulative scheme and renewed findings that continued suspension was justified in the public interest. A shareholder of CJL brought suit, challenging the commission's authority under section 12(k) to suspend the trading of securities beyond ten days summarily through the use of "tacking" orders. Rejecting the assertion that the suit was moot because the commission's suspension orders had terminated, the court of appeals held that section 12(k) did not authorize the commission to issue successive orders to curtail trading in a security in excess of ten days.

Questions: (1) Was the suit moot because of the termination of the questioned suspension orders? (2) Does section 12(k) empower the commission to issue a series of summary orders, on the basis of a single alleged manipulative scheme, to suspend trading beyond ten days?

Decision: No to both questions. Opinion by Justice Rehnquist. Vote: 9–0, Brennan, Marshall, and Blackmun concurring in the judgment.

Reasons: A federal lawsuit is not moot if it challenges action of too short duration to be fully litigated prior to the cessation or expiration of the action and there is a reasonable expectation that the complaining party will again be confronted with the contested action. The attack on the commission's use of section 12(k) satisfies the first part of the test because a series of summary suspension orders may last no more than 20 days. The second part is also satisfied because CLJ's recurrent violations of the securities laws make it reasonably likely that its shareholders will be injured by a renewed series of suspension orders under section 12(k).

Turning to the merits, the language of section 12(k) expressly confines a summary suspension order to "a period not exceeding ten days." Only a clear mandate from Congress could justify an interpretation that would circumvent this restriction because "the power to summarily suspend trading in a security even for ten days, without any notice, opportunity to be heard or findings based on a record, is an awesome power with a potentially devastating impact on the issuer, its shareholders, and other investors." No such mandate can be found. The procedural protections offered to issuers registering securities and to brokers and dealers before long-term suspensions can be ordered, moreover, reinforces the conclusion that section 12(k) power, shorn of procedural safeguards, cannot be extended beyond ten days.

Although the commission's interpretation of the summary suspension power authorized by section 12(k) is entitled to some deference, it cannot defeat express statutory language without persuasive legislative history or compelling reasons of policy to buttress its view.

Duke Power Co. v. Carolina Environmental Study Group, Inc., 438 U.S. 59 (1978)

Facts: Seeking to stop the construction of nuclear power plants by the Duke Power Company, an environmental organization, a labor union, and persons residing close to the planned facilities sued the privately owned utility and the Nuclear Regulatory Commission (NRC) to obtain a declaratory judgment that the Price-Anderson Act, 42 U.S. Code 2210, is unconstitutional. To encourage the development of the nuclear power industry, the act limits aggregate tort liability for a single nuclear accident to $560 million: $315 million to be paid by nuclear plant licensees, $140 million from private insurance, and the remaining $105 million assumed by the federal government. Plaintiffs contended that the due process clause of the Fifth Amendment offers a private right of action to attack arbitrary legislation that threatens property rights, that the Price-Anderson Act was arbitrary because it failed to guarantee adequate compensation to victims of nuclear accidents, and that the act threatened plaintiffs' right to fair compensation in the event of an accident, because without its protection nuclear power plants would not be built. In addition, plaintiffs alleged that the operation of Duke Power's nuclear power plants would cause them injury in the form of exposure to radiation and thermal pollution of two recreational lakes. After finding a substantial likelihood that Duke Power's nuclear plants would be neither completed nor operated absent the Price-Anderson Act, the district court struck down the $560 million ceiling on liability as irrational under the due process clause. The court concluded that the ceiling was not reasonably related to potential losses caused by nuclear accidents, it encouraged irresponsibility with respect to safety and the environment, and it offered no quid pro quo for limiting the rights of recovery at common law of accident victims.

Questions: (1) Did the district court have subject matter jurisdiction over the lawsuit? (2) Did plaintiffs have standing? (3) Was the case ripe for adjudication? (4) Is the Price-Anderson Act unconstitutional?

Decision: Yes to questions 1–3 and no to question 4. Opinion by Chief Justice Burger. Votes: 7–2, 6–2, 6–2, and 9–0, respectively, Stewart concurring in the result, Rehnquist and Stevens concurring in the judgment.

Reasons: The district court had jurisdiction over the suit against the Nuclear Regulatory Commission (NRC) under 28 U.S. Code 1331(a). That provision confers jurisdiction over claims founded on the Constitution and asserted against federal agencies without regard to the amount in controversy. The NRC was sued because it is charged with the enforcement and administration of the Price-Anderson Act. Plaintiffs' due process claim for relief against the NRC under the Fifth Amendment had sufficient substance to sustain the exercise of subject-matter jurisdiction.

The plaintiffs' standing was properly established on the basis of findings that were not clearly erroneous. The district court found that the operation of Duke Power's nuclear plants would cause the plaintiffs environmental, aesthetic, and physical injury. In addition, it concluded that constitutional condemnation of the Price-Anderson Act would probably remedy these injuries because nuclear power plants would be neither built nor operated without the $560 million ceiling on liability. Once such a causal link between injury and the challenged conduct has been shown, the requirements of Article III of the Constitution with respect to standing are satisfied, at least outside the context of suits by taxpayers. Article III does not require any logical or additional connection between the injuries alleged and the constitutional rights asserted.

The lawsuit was ripe for adjudication, both because plaintiffs' alleged injuries were immediate and because a decision on the merits would remove a source of debilitating uncertainty from the nuclear power industry.

The Price-Anderson Act is a type of economic regulation that satisfies due process scrutiny if it is rationally related to a legitimate goal. Its $560 million ceiling on liability advances the nation's legitimate interest in fostering the development of nuclear power. It offers no incentive for inattention to concerns of safety because nuclear power plants must satisfy a host of federal safety standards. Finally, by establishing strict liability for nuclear accidents and guaranteeing payments to victims of at least $560 million (irrespective of the solvency of the licensee of a nuclear power plant), the Price-Anderson Act offers a reasonably fair substitute for the remedies under the common or state tort law that it displaces.

Vermont Yankee Nuclear Power v. Natural Resources Defense Council, 435 U.S. 519 (1978)

Facts: The Vermont Yankee Nuclear Power Corporation applied to the Atomic Energy Commission (AEC) for a license to operate a nuclear power plant.[21] A hearing was held to explore the environmental impact of the license pursuant to the National Environmental Policy Act (NEPA), but consideration of the environmental effects of the reprocessing of nuclear fuel and the disposal of nuclear waste was excluded. Thereafter, the commission instituted rulemaking proceedings to consider the environmental effects associated with the uranium fuel cycle. Ultimately it promulgated a rule requiring an environmental evaluation of fuel reprocessing and waste disposal in determining whether to grant a license to operate a nuclear plant. But since these environmental effects are on the whole insignificant, the commission reasoned, it was unnecessary to require retroactive application of the rule to the grant of Vermont Yankee's application for a license.

Consumers Power Company sought a permit from the AEC to construct two nuclear reactors in Midland, Michigan. Extensive hearings were held on the environmental implications of granting the permit, but the commission declined to make a detailed inquiry as to whether energy-conservation measures might obviate the necessity of the reactors. This decision was founded largely on the failure of environmental groups that were opposed to the permit to suggest any conservation alternatives that might plausibly curtail demand for a significant amount of electricity. The construction permit was granted.

The orders of the AEC granting Vermont Yankee an operating license and Consumers Power a construction permit were challenged in the court of appeals. With regard to the former, the court held that the commission had failed to follow adequate procedures in its rulemaking proceedings concerning the environmental effects of the reprocessing of nuclear fuel and the disposal of nuclear wastes. The latter order was condemned for failure to examine conservation of

---

[21] In the course of litigation of these cases, the licensing and regulatory functions of the AEC were transferred to the Nuclear Regulatory Commission (NRC) by the Energy Reorganization Act of 1974.

energy as an alternative to the nuclear plants and for asserted deficiencies in a safety report issued by the Advisory Committee on
Reactor Safeguards (ACRS) and incorporated in the permit application.

Question: Did the court of appeals intrude on administrative discretion improperly in overturning the orders of the AEC?

Decision: Yes. Opinion by Justice Rehnquist. Vote: 7–0. Blackmun
and Powell did not participate.

Reasons: The court of appeals chastised the AEC for not offering
sufficient opportunities to participate in its rulemaking proceedings
regarding the nuclear fuel cycle. In so doing, the court failed to adhere
to the well-established principle that administrative agencies possess
broad discretion under the Administrative Procedure Act (APA) to
fashion rules of procedure and methods of inquiry appropriate to the
discharge of their multitudinous duties. The court of appeals did not
find that the AEC had strayed from the rulemaking procedures required by 5 U.S. Code 553, but thought it proper to impose additional
requirements when questions having to do with the NEPA are at
stake. The NEPA, however, does not repeal any other statute by
implication and offers no foundation for revising the procedural requirements of the APA.

> In short, nothing in the APA, NEPA, the circumstances of
> this case, the nature of the issues being considered, past
> agency practice, or the statutory mandate under which the
> commission operates permitted the court to review and
> overturn the rulemaking proceeding on the basis of the pro-
> cedural devices employed . . . by the commission so long as
> [it] employed at least the statutory minima.

The court of appeals also erred in condemning as arbitrary and
capricious the AEC's failure to examine conservation of energy as an
alternative to the nuclear plants proposed by Consumers Power.
Administrative bodies are obliged under the NEPA to develop detailed statements on alternatives to proposed action having significant
environmental implications. The term *alternatives* however, is not self-
defining. Common sense teaches that it does not embrace

> every alternative device and thought conceivable by the
> mind of man. Time and resources are simply too limited to
> hold that an [environmental] impact statement fails because
> the agency failed to ferret out every possible alternative,
> regardless of how uncommon or unknown that alternative

may have been at the time the project was approved. . . . [T]he concept of "alternatives" is an evolving one, requiring the agency to explore more or fewer alternatives as they become better known and understood.

In this case, Consumer Power's construction permit was considered before the drastic oil shortages of 1973 and before conservation of energy had had a significant impact on the thinking of the public. Nothing in the record before the AEC, moreover, including the comments by environmental groups opposed to the application, indicated that the nuclear project would be unnecessary in order to satisfy the demand for electricity. In these circumstances, the AEC acted well within its discretion in declining to examine conservation of energy as an alternative to the nuclear power plants.

Finally, the finding by the court of appeals of deficiencies in the safety report of the ACRS represented "judicial intervention run riot." The report was flawed, said the court of appeals, because its language was not understandable to a layman, a remarkable finding in view of the failure of any member of the supposedly uncomprehending public to request a revision of the report. The court lacked any authority to command the commission or the ACRS to explain in layman's language each generic safety concern raised by a nuclear reactor.

> Nuclear energy may some day be a cheap, safe source of power or it may not. But Congress has made a choice to at least try nuclear energy, establishing a reasonable review process in which courts are to play only a limited role. The fundamental policy questions appropriately resolved in Congress and in the state legislatures are *not* subject to reexamination in the federal courts under the guise of judicial review of agency action.

Tennessee Valley Authority v. *Hill,* 437 U.S. 153 (1978)

Facts: In 1967, Congress appropriated initial funds for the construction of the Tellico Dam and Reservoir Project located on the Little Tennessee River. In 1973, Congress passed the Endangered Species Act, which empowers the secretary of the interior to list species of animal life that are in danger of extinction and to identify their "critical habitat." Once a species or its habitat is listed, the act commands all federal departments or agencies to conduct their operations so as to avoid jeopardizing the continued existence of the species or destroying or modifying its habitat.

In 1975, when the Tellico Dam was nearly complete, the secretary listed the snail darter as an endangered species. He also determined that the snail darter apparently lived only in that portion of the Little Tennessee River which would be inundated by the impoundment of water behind the dam and that the reservoir thus created would destroy the fish's critical habitat.

In 1976, private parties filed suit seeking to enjoin completion of the dam and impoundment of the reservoir on the ground that such actions would cause the extinction of the snail darter in violation of the act. The district court found that the plaintiffs' legal claim was valid, but declined to issue an injunction. It reasoned that Congress had repeatedly appropriated funds for the Tellico Dam with knowledge of the problem of the snail darter and could not have intended to abort a decade-long hundred-million-dollar project in passing the act. Reversing the denial of an injunction, the court of appeals concluded that the act compelled this result whether or not millions of dollars of public funds were irretrievably lost as a consequence.

Question: Does the Endangered Species Act require enjoining the completion and operation of the Tellico Dam to preserve the snail darter and its critical habitat?

Decision: Yes. Opinion by Chief Justice Burger. Vote: 6–3, Powell, Blackmun, and Rehnquist dissenting.

Reasons: The language and legislative history of the act disclose an unequivocal intent of Congress to "halt and reverse the trend toward species extinction, whatever the cost." Congress anticipated that vindication of the policies embodied in the act might require aborting or modifying federal projects already under way. It nevertheless chose to subordinate these losses to what it perceived to be the greater value of an endangered species. Accordingly, the act cannot countenance the completion and operation of the Tellico Dam, since the existence of the dam would jeopardize the continued existence of the snail darter and its critical habitat.

The enactment of appropriations measures for the Tellico Dam after the snail darter was listed does not undermine this conclusion. It is a cardinal rule of construction that a later statute will be interpreted to repeal an earlier statute by implication only if the two are irreconcilable. The subsequent appropriations measures were arguably the offspring of confident assertions by the TVA that efforts to transplant the snail darter and avoid collision with the act would be successful. Consequently, they are reconcilable with the act.

136

By invoking equitable considerations to justify withholding equitable relief, the district court displayed infidelity to the clear mandate of Congress and the separation of powers. "Once the meaning of an enactment is discerned and its constitutionality determined, the judicial process comes to an end."

Parker v. *Flook,* 437 U.S. 584 (1978)

Facts: Flook sought a patent on a method of periodically updating so-called alarm limits during catalytic chemical conversion of hydrocarbons. If certain variables exceed the limit, an alarm may signal the presence of an abnormal condition to indicate either inefficiency or perhaps danger. The updating formula is useful primarily for computerized calculations that produce automatic adjustments in settings of the alarm. The patent office rejected the application on the ground that the formula was ineligible for protection under section 101 of the Patent Act. The Court of Customs and Patent Appeals reversed.

Question: Is the applicant's mathematical formula for periodic updating of alarm limits eligible for patent protection?

Decision: No. Opinion by Justice Stevens. Vote: 6–3, Stewart, Burger, and Rehnquist dissenting.

Reasons: Section 101 of the Patent Act describes the types of discoveries or inventions that may qualify for patent protection and embraces any "new and useful process." A mathematical algorithm was declared an unpatentable process in *Gottshalk* v. *Benson,* 409 U.S. 63 (1972). The reasoning in that case and in *O'Reilly* v. *Morse,* 15 HOW 62 (1853), support the conclusion that a method of calculation pursuant to a mathematical formula, no matter how specific its purpose, is not patentable under section 101. This decision does not reflect:

> a judgment that patent protection of certain novel and useful computer programs will not promote the progress of science and the useful arts. . . . Difficult questions of policy concerning the kinds of programs that may be appropriate for patent protection and the form and duration of such protection can be answered by Congress on the basis of current empirical data not equally available to this tribunal.

State Taxation and Regulation of Commerce

Riding the crest of growing dissatisfaction with government regulation, the Court struck down during the 1977–1978 term three state laws that curtailed business freedom. On the other hand, a state statute insulating gasoline retailers from competition offered by vertically integrated oil companies was held to be beyond constitutional reproach. And New York City was absolved of any constitutional obligation to pay just compensation for the depreciated value of Grand Central Terminal caused by its designation as a historic landmark. Finally, the Court sympathetically embraced state measures to increase tax collections in four decisions in which attacks on their constitutionality were rejected.

Contract Clause. Article I, Section 10, clause 1 of the Constitution speaks, in part, with deceptive simplicity: "No State shall . . . pass any . . . law impairing the obligation of contracts." Lurking behind this injunction, however, are a multiplicity of competing values that have yielded decisions that are difficult to reconcile. Generally speaking, in application of the contract clause accommodation of both the legitimate expectations of contracting parties and the need of the state to legislate in the public interest has been sought. Until recent years, the former interest was ordinarily subordinated to the latter. In *United States Trust Co. of New York* v. *New Jersey*, 431 U.S. 1 (1977), however, the Court indicated that it was reversing its sympathies. There it held that the repeal of a statutory covenant whose initial enactment was intended to protect the security of bondholders offended the contract clause. This term, the decision in *Allied Structural Steel Co.* v. *Spannaus*, 438 U.S. 234 (1978), confirmed that the Court is offering enhanced protection of private contractual expectations in expounding the restraints that the contract clause imposes on state legislation. The facts of the case were as follows:

In 1973, Allied voluntarily adopted a pension plan for its employees, reserving the right to amend or terminate the plan at any time and to distribute the assets of the pension fund pursuant to a prescribed formula. Substantial pension benefits were vested only if rigorous standards as to age and duration of employment were satisfied, and Allied was not obliged to make annual contributions to the pension fund. More than a decade later, Minnesota enacted a law by which charges were assessed against employers who terminated pension plans or closed offices without guaranteeing full pensions to all employees who had worked at least ten years. Upon closing an office in Minnesota, Allied was assessed a pension funding charge of $185,000.

Writing for a 5–3 majority, Justice Stewart declared that the assessment must give way to the employer's legitimate contractual expectation that his pension liabilities would not exceed those for which he had bargained privately. The contract clause, Stewart said, protects the private ordering of business affairs against unanticipated and severe disruption by the state. The Minnesota law, he continued, constituted a frontal assault on Allied's private plan for satisfying pension obligations. It exposed Allied retroactively to $185,000 in additional pension charges with no time for phasing in the new obligations. Moreover, Stewart observed, the pension law was not the offspring of any urgent economic or social problem demanding immediate attention. Accordingly, Stewart concluded, the contract clause could not countenance Minnesota's impairment of Allied's contractual pension obligations.

Whether the *Allied Structural Steel* decision portends a wholesale redirection of jurisprudence with reference to the contract clause is problematic. Stewart offered this cryptic characterization of the ruling: "[W]e do hold that if the Contract Clause means anything at all, it means that Minnesota could not constitutionally do what it tried to do to the company in this case."

Commerce Clause. Justice Cardozo eloquently explained the general intolerance under the commerce clause of state statutes that encumber national economic markets:

> To give entrance to [protectionism] would be to invite a speedy end of our national solidarity. The Constitution was framed under the dominion of a political philosophy less parochial in range. It was framed upon the theory that the peoples of the several states must sink or swim together, and that in the long run prosperity and salvation are in union and not division. *Baldwin* v. *G.A.F. Seelig*, 294 U.S. 511 at 523 (1935).

Bowing to this philosophy in *City of Philadelphia* v. *New Jersey*, 437 U.S. 617 (1978), the Court overturned a New Jersey statute that prohibited the importation of solid or liquid waste which originated or was collected outside the territorial limits of the state. Writing for a 7–2 majority, Justice Stewart observed that the effect of the statute was to reserve the state's landfill space solely to commercial interests within the state. In seeking to isolate itself from a common problem of refuse disposal, Stewart explained, New Jersey had erected a barrier against interstate disposal of domestic wastes. The commerce clause, he concluded, was intended to forestall such acts of economic isolationism.

In *Raymond Motor Transportation, Inc.* v. *Rice*, 434 U.S. 429 (1978), the Court swept aside a state law that banned the use of sixty-five-foot double trailer units and thereby impeded the efficiency of interstate trucking. The commerce clause, said the Court, condemned this burden on interstate commerce, since the contested state law was not shown to contribute to highway safety. In stark contrast to the decisions in *Philadelphia* and *Raymond Motor*, state barriers to interstate competition were greeted sympathetically in *Exxon Corporation* v. *Governor of Maryland*, 437 U.S. 117 (1978). There the Court upheld a Maryland law that prohibited producers or refiners of petroleum from retailing gasoline and obliged them to price uniformly in supplying service stations. The law stemmed from complaints by independent retailers that the large, vertically integrated oil companies favored their own stations in times of short supply. Its divestiture effects on the retail market were visited almost exclusively on businesses outside Maryland, since no producers or refiners of petroleum are located in the state. Nevertheless, the Court held, the law did not offend the commerce clause because it offered no preference to instate marketers of gasoline over their interstate rivals and because regulatory uniformity was unnecessary to protect the interstate flow of gasoline. With regard to the statutory command of price uniformity in supplying retailers, the Court rejected the claim that it was pre-empted by federal antitrust laws that favor price competition. There was no irreconcilable conflict between the state and federal statutes, the Court explained, and an adverse effect on competition alone is insufficient to taint state regulation under the doctrine of pre-emption.

Just Compensation. Scores of laws have been enacted in recent years that are designed to preserve historic landmarks from demolition or alteration threatened by private commercial or residential development. Restricting the development of landmark buildings or sites depresses their economic value to the detriment of the economic interests of owners. If the government resists paying for this depression in value, the injured owners arguably have constitutional claims for just compensation under the Fifth Amendment. If the claims are sustained, the entire community, rather than only a few, must undertake the economic burden of preserving our cultural heritage.

In *Penn Central Transportation Co.* v. *City of New York*, 438 U.S. 104 (1978), the Court addressed a just compensation claim advanced by the owner of Grand Central Terminal, Penn Central. New York City had designated the terminal as a historic landmark, thereby activating restrictions on its commercial development. After unsuccessfully seeking city approval to build a multilevel office building atop the terminal, Penn Central brought suit, claiming that the city had effected an unconstitutional taking of its property by curtailing Grand Central's development opportunities. The Supreme Court, speaking through Justice Brennan, disagreed.

Brennan noted that Penn Central could operate the terminal at a reasonable profit without any further development. Moreover, he observed, New York City empowered Penn Central to transfer commercial development rights from the terminal to at least eight other nearby parcels it owned. Finally, Brennan explained, the law did not preclude the possibility of commercial development of the terminal in ways that would not threaten its character as a historic landmark. In these circumstances, Brennan concluded, no constitutional taking of Penn Central's property had occurred.

Although the holding in Penn Central was narrowly tailored to the facts, it seems to contain several broader teachings. First, a landmark law is not constitutionally flawed simply because it sharply depresses the market value of property. Second, it need not impose identical or similar restrictions on all structures or sites within its preservative ambit to escape constitutional condemnation. Third, landmark laws can avoid exacting constitutional scrutiny if they offer no direct fiscal advantages to the government.

Taxation. Discarding a forty-year old ruling, the Court handed a victory to state revenue officials by endorsing a state occupation tax on stevedoring in *Department of Revenue of the State of Washington* v. *Association of Washington Stevedoring Companies*, 435 U.S. 734 (1978). In 1937, the Court had invalidated a virtually identical tax under the commerce clause. That decision was founded on the view that stevedoring activities are integral to interstate commerce and that to tax the activities would thus be tantamount to an impermissible tax on interstate commerce itself. Its theoretical foundation was removed, however, in *Complete Auto Transit, Inc.* v. *Brady*, 430 U.S. 274 (1977). There the Court concluded that the commerce clause could countenance state taxes on interstate businesses "when the tax is applied to an activity with a substantial nexus with the taxing State, is fairly apportioned, does not discriminate against interstate commerce, and is fairly related to the services provided by the State." Since the contested stevedoring tax in *Association of Washington Stevedoring Co.* met the standards of *Complete Auto*, the Court held that it contained no infirmity under the commerce clause. The decades-old *Stevedoring Cases*, which pointed in the other direction, the Court declared, are overruled. The Court also rejected the argument that the stevedoring occupation tax was tantamount to a tax on imports and exports and was thus prohibited by the import-export clause, Article I, Section 10, clause 2.

Spurred by the problems of taxing multistate businesses, a score of states joined the Multistate Tax Compact to facilitate the proper determination of tax liabilities, promote uniformity in state taxing systems, lessen the paperwork of tax administration, and avoid duplicative taxation. The compact created the Multistate Tax Commission, which is empowered to perform audits at the request of a member state and to use the compulsory process authority of any consenting state.

Threatened with an audit by the commission, several large multistate businesses brought suit, challenging the constitutionality of the Multistate Tax Compact. The cornerstone of their attack was that the member states had entered into an agreement or compact without the consent of Congress as required by Article 1, Section 10, clause 3 of the Constitution—the compact clause. It provides that "No State shall, without the consent of Congress . . . enter into any Agreement or Compact with another State." A 7–2 majority rejected the constitutional attack in *United States Steel Corp.* v. *Multistate Tax Commission*, 434 U.S. 452 (1978).

Writing for the Court, Justice Powell explained that an agreement is within the ambit of the compact clause only if it enhances the power of a state at the expense of federal authority. Since the Multistate Tax Compact neither empowered states to exercise any authority they could not otherwise exercise nor curtailed their freedom to impose or collect taxes, it was beyond the scope of the compact clause.

Multistate businesses were also unsuccessful in seeking constitutional shelter from state taxation in *Moorman Manufacturing Co.* v. *Bair*, 437 U.S. 267 (1978). At issue was the application of an Iowa corporate income tax to the income of an interstate business that was derived from the manufacture and sale of tangible personal property. The presumption behind the questioned statute was that the portion of income attributable to business transacted in Iowa was the proportion of total gross sales that were made in Iowa. Neither due process nor the commerce clause, the Court held, justifies invalidating this presumption.

The march of recreational hunters towards Montana's elk produced a constitutional confrontation in *Baldwin* v. *Fish and Game Commission of Montana*, 436 U.S. 371 (1978). The Montana hunting-license system imposes on nonresidents an elk-hunting license fee several times as high as the fee imposed on residents. Unfurling the privileges and immunities clause of Article IV, Section 2, and the equal protection clause of the Fourteenth Amendment, nonresident elk hunters marched into federal court seeking to condemn the discrimination in licensing rates. Justice Blackmun, speaking for a 6–3 majority, concluded that the privileges and immunities clause offers no protection against discrimination embedded in the regulation of recreational hunting. And differences in state taxes paid by residents and nonresidents, Blackmun added, justifies the exaction of higher license fees from the latter in order to offset the cost to the state of maintaining preserves of elk and other wildlife. The license-fee differential, he thus concluded, passes equal protection scrutiny.

Allied Structural Steel Company v. *Spannaus*, 438 U.S. 234 (1978)

Facts: In 1963, an Illinois corporation with a thirty-employee office in Minnesota, Allied, voluntarily adopted a companywide pension plan. The plan offered benefits only to employees who retired at the age of sixty-five or satisfied three exacting conditions turning on years of employment with the company and age. It did not oblige Allied to fund vested pension benefits and permitted termination of the pension trust fund that received Allied's voluntary contributions at any time and for any reason. In the event of termination, all assets of the fund would be distributed pursuant to a specified plan, thereby discharging all Allied's pension obligations. More than a decade after the adoption of the plan Minnesota enacted a law that assessed any private employer of a hundred or more employees, at least one of whom was a resident of Minnesota, a pension-funding charge if the employer either terminated a pension plan or closed a Minnesota office without guaranteeing full pensions to all employees who had worked for more than ten years. Allied was assessed a $185,000 pension funding charge when it discharged eleven Minnesota employees in the process of closing its Minnesota office. It urged unsuccessfully in federal district court that the contract clause of the Constitution invalidated the assessment because it unexpectedly and significantly broadened Allied's contractual pension obligations.

Question: Did the contract clause, Article I, Section 10, clause 1, shield Allied from the financial burden of Minnesota's pension-funding charge?

Decision: Yes. Opinion by Justice Stewart. Vote: 5–3, Brennan, White, and Marshall dissenting. Blackmun did not participate.

Reasons: The contract clause shields private contracts from impairment by state legislation. In decisions expounding the clause no bright-line test for determining its reach has been established. The greater the general public interests advanced by a statute, the greater the disruption of private contractual expectations that the contract clause will countenance.

In this case, the contested Minnesota statute upset Allied's legitimate contractual expectations, which had governed its pension planning for ten years, by unexpectedly raising its obligations by $185,000. This severe disruption of contractual expectations was not necessary in order to meet an important social problem. The statute was not an emergency measure; it entered a field never before regulated by the state, and it was narrowly aimed only at large private employers with voluntary pension plans who either terminated their plans or closed Minnesota offices. Whatever public interests that statute was designed to serve were insufficient to justify its nullification of Allied's contractual pension obligations by the imposition of an unexpected additional $185,000 charge.

City of Philadelphia v. *New Jersey*, 437 U.S. 617 (1978)

Facts: A New Jersey law prohibits the importation of most "solid or liquid waste which originated or was collected outside the territorial limits of the State." Several cities and operators of private landfills in New Jersey brought suit, claiming that the law was constitutionally infirm under the commerce clause, Article I, Section 8, clause 3. Finding that the law advanced vital health and environmental objectives, the New Jersey Supreme Court held it invulnerable to attack under the commerce clause.

Question: Does New Jersey's discrimination against out-of-state waste in the allocation of its private landfill areas offend the commerce clause?

Decision: Yes. Opinion by Justice Stewart. Vote: 7–2, Rehnquist and Burger dissenting.

Reasons: The commerce clause demands that states adhere to a principle of nondiscrimination in the regulation of interstate commerce, whether their objectives are the health of their residents, protection of the environment, or others. This principle is affronted by the contested New Jersey law, which placed the full burden of conserving the state's remaining private landfill space on commerce in out-of-state waste. The commerce clause cannot countenance New

Jersey's attempt "to isolate itself from a problem common to many by erecting a barrier against the movement of interstate trade."

Past decisions sustaining state power to ban the importation of diseased livestock or other articles whose transport endangers health cannot save the New Jersey law. The dangers to health hazards and the environment that are traceable to out-of-state waste arise after its disposal in landfill sites and are indistinguishable from the threats posed by domestic waste.

Raymond Motor Transportation, Inc. v. Rice, 434 U.S. 429 (1978)

Facts: Denied permission to use sixty-five-foot double trailer units on Wisconsin highways, an interstate trucker attacked the administrative regulations invoked to thwart his operations as an unconstitutional burden on interstate commerce. The regulations generally limit vehicles pulling a single trailer to an overall length of fifty-five feet and proscribe the use of double trailer units. At trial, the trucker offered undisputed evidence that sixty-five-foot doubles are as safe to operate as fifty-five-foot singles and that increased costs, slower service, and disruption of interstate trucking could be ascribed to the challenged regulations. The district court, however, found no infirmity under the commerce clause in the regulations. It reasoned that sixty-five-foot doubles are more dangerous than fifty-five-foot singles because the former take longer for a motorist to pass. Accordingly, the district court concluded, the regulations advance a sufficiently strong state interest to justify its burden on interstate trucking.

Question: Do the contested state regulations as applied to prohibit use of sixty-five-foot doubles by an interstate trucker offend the commerce clause, Article I, Section 8, clause 3 of the Constitution?

Decision: Yes. Opinion by Justice Powell. Vote: 8–0. Stevens did not participate.

Reasons: The commerce clause shields interstate commerce from excessive interference or discrimination by the states. The constitutional framework for evaluating a commerce clause attack on a nondiscriminatory state statute was expressed in *Pike* v. *Bruce Church, Inc.*, 397 U.S. 137 (1970):

> Where the statute regulates evenhandedly to effectuate a legitimate local public interest, and its effects on interstate commerce are only incidental, it will be upheld unless the

145

burden imposed on such commerce is clearly excessive in relation to the putative local benefits.

In the field of highway safety, great deference should be paid to state regulations. In this case, however, there was undisputed evidence to show that sixty-five-foot doubles are as safe as fifty-five-foot singles. Evidence was adduced to establish that the difference in passing time posed no appreciable hazard to motorists. In addition the state offered a maze of exemptions from the fifty-five-foot limit that were principally of benefit to local industry. These facts undermine the contention that the highway regulations are truly safety measures.

The regulations substantially increase the cost of interstate trucking, moreover, and slow the movement of goods. To comply, truckers must either haul double trailers across the state separately, bypass the state, or incur the delays caused by using singles instead of doubles to pick up and deliver goods. In addition, interstate truckers are prevented from accepting interline transfers from carriers operating in the thirty-three states where the doubles are legal.

Finally, the preference accorded local industry by the regulations removes an important political check on undue burdens on interstate commerce that is raised when state laws operate without discrimination.

On this record, we are persuaded that the challenged regulations violated the Commerce Clause because they place a substantial burden on interstate commerce and they cannot be said to make more than the most speculative contribution to highway safety.

Exxon Corporation v. Governor of Maryland, 437 U.S. 117 (1978)

Facts: Responding to complaints of inequitable distribution of gasoline among retail stations in the wake of the 1973 Arab oil embargo, Maryland enacted a statute that prohibits any producer or refiner of petroleum products from operating any retail gasoline station within the state. The statute also requires that price discounts be offered uniformly to all service stations supplied by the producer or refiner. Exxon and several other producers and refiners of petroleum products that were required by the statute to divest themselves of their retail stations challenged its constitutionality in state court. First, it was urged that the statute offended substantive due process, because it would thwart rather than enhance competition. Second, the commerce clause was said to condemn the statute, because virtually all the producers and refiners that were required to divest resided outside Maryland. Finally, it was argued, the uniform pricing policy of the statute was pre-empted by section 2(b) of the Robinson-Patman Act. The Maryland Court of Appeals rejected the attacks.

Questions: (1) Does the statute violate the due process clause of the Fourteenth Amendment? (2) Do its divestiture provisions violate the commerce clause? (3) Is the uniform pricing provision pre-empted by the Robinson-Patman Act?

Decision: No to all questions. Votes: 8–0, 7–1, 8–0, respectively, Blackmun dissenting in part. Powell did not participate.

Reasons: Substantive due process does not shelter business from statutes that may have anticompetitive effects. The contested divestiture provision was the offspring of evidence that producers and refiners were favoring company-operated stations in the allocation of gasoline and that such favoritism would ultimately reduce competition in the retail market. Whether or not the provision proves to be anticompetitive, it is sufficiently related to the state's legitimate purpose in controlling the retail gasoline market to satisfy substantive due process scrutiny.

The statute is likewise beyond reproach under the commerce clause. It neither discriminates against interstate commerce nor favors local producers or refiners of gasoline, since none are located in Maryland. Local retailers are not favored because their interstate competitors, which operate solely at the retail level, are beneficiaries of the statute. In addition, the statute does not impermissibly burden interstate commerce, because it threatens no diminution of total gasoline supplies from interstate refiners. If some refiners that are subject to divestiture cease supplying the Maryland market, their business will be shifted to their interstate competitors. Finally, national uniformity in the regulation of retail gasoline sales is not required in order to forestall state laws that might impede the interstate flow of petroleum products. Accordingly, the free-market policies fostered by the commerce clause are not jeopardized by the questioned statute.

The uniform pricing policy mandated by the statute neither directly conflicts with section 2(b) of the Robinson-Patman Act nor frustrates the basic federal policy in favor of competition. Although there are hypothetical situations in which the statute may command a uniform pricing policy where the federal act would permit price discrimination, this sort of hypothetical conflict does not warrant pre-emption. Similarly, the well-settled principle disfavoring pre-emption of state police powers forecloses the argument that the statute runs afoul of the competitive pricing policies endorsed by the Sherman and Robinson-Patman acts. Its uniform-pricing mandate may impede competition, but "if an adverse effect on competition were, in and of itself, enough to render a state statute invalid, the States' power to engage in economic regulation would be effectively destroyed."

Penn Central Transportation Co. v. *City of New York,* 438 U.S. 104 (1978)

Facts: As part of a comprehensive program to preserve historic landmarks and historic districts, the New York City Landmarks Law places more exacting restrictions on the development of individual historic landmarks than those imposed by zoning ordinances. The owner of a landmark must keep exterior features of the building in good repair and cannot alter the features or construct any exterior improvement without the approval of the Landmarks Preservation Commission. Alterations or improvements are permitted only if they will neither change any architectural feature of the landmark nor hinder its protection and use unduly. The owner of a landmark, however, may transfer commercial development rights that are available under applicable ordinances to parcels that it owns on nearby streets.

Grand Central Terminal was designated as one of 400 individual historic landmarks under the Landmarks Law. Its owner, Penn Central, was denied permission to construct a fifty-five-story office building atop the terminal because it would destroy its aesthetic value. Penn Central then brought suit in state court contending that application of the Landmarks Law to deny commercial development of the terminal constituted a "taking" of its property without just compensation, in violation of the Fifth and Fourteenth amendments, and deprived Penn Central of its property without due process of law, in contravention of the Fourteenth Amendment. Noting Penn Central's failure to show that it could not earn a reasonable return on its investment in the terminal and noting that valuable development rights could be transferred to other Penn Central properties, the New York Court of Appeals rejected the constitutional attack.

Question: Did application of the Landmarks Law to restrict development of Grand Central Terminal by Penn Central effect an unconstitutional taking of property under the Fifth Amendment and deprive Penn Central of its property without due process of law under the Fourteenth Amendment?

Decision: No. Opinion by Justice Brennan. Vote: 6–3, Rehnquist, Burger, and Stevens dissenting.

Reasons: The Fifth Amendment enjoins the government from taking private property for public use without just compensation. Its purpose is to bar the government from requiring persons or groups to shoulder public burdens which, in all fairness and justice, should be borne by the public as a whole. When government acts to promote health, safety, morals, or the general welfare, concomitant economic harms that it inflicts on a reasonably broad class do not constitute a taking if the harms are necessary to the effectuation of the government goal.

In this case, the Landmarks Law was an appropriate means of advancing New York City's legitimate objective of preserving structures and areas with special historic, architectural, or cultural significance. Although it diminished the economic value of the terminal, approximately 400 other properties were comparably disadvantaged. In addition, the diminution was in part offset by the availability to Penn Central of transfer development rights and did not deny Penn Central a reasonable return on its investment in the terminal. Finally, Penn Central may further develop the terminal if it can devise a plan that would not unduly denigrate the value of the terminal as a landmark. These considerations compel the conclusion that the Landmarks Law did not effect a taking of Penn Central's property.

Department of Revenue of the State of Washington v. Association of Washington Stevedoring Companies, 435 U.S. 734 (1978)

Facts: An association of stevedoring companies challenged the constitutionality of a business and occupation tax imposed by the state of Washington on stevedoring—the business of loading and unloading cargo from ships. The commerce clause, Article I, Section 8, clause 3, and the import-export clause, Article I, Section 10, clause 2, it was urged, shield the business of stevedoring from state taxation because of its inseparable relation to interstate and foreign commerce. Relying on *Puget Sound Stevedoring Co. v. State Tax Commission,* 302 U.S. 90 (1937), and *Joseph v. Carter & Weeks Stevedoring Co.,* 330 U.S. 422 (1937) (*Stevedoring Cases*), in which virtually identical state taxes on stevedoring had been condemned, the Supreme Court of Washington held the questioned tax unconstitutional.

Question: Does either the commerce clause or the import-export clause prohibit states from imposing a nondiscriminatory business and occupation tax on stevedoring?

Decision: No. Opinion by Justice Blackmun. Vote: 8–0, Powell concurring in part and concurring in the result. Brennan did not participate.

Reasons: The *Stevedoring Cases* were founded on the principle that the commerce clause cannot countenance state taxes on gross receipts that are imposed directly on the privilege of engaging in interstate commerce. Stevedoring was viewed as a part of interstate commerce itself. The decision in *Complete Auto Transit, Inc.* v. *Brady,* 430 U.S. 274 (1977), however, disavowed the principle underpinning the *Stevedoring Cases.* In *Complete Auto* it was held that a state may levy a fairly apportioned and nondiscriminatory tax on the gross receipts of an interstate business without offending the commerce clause. That clause, *Complete Auto* concluded, shields interstate activities from taxes that threaten multiple burdens of the type intrastate business can avoid, but it does not relieve those engaged in interstate commerce from paying their just share of state taxes, even though it increases the cost to them of doing business. The tax under challenge here was levied solely on the value of loading and unloading that occurred in Washington and thus threatened no multiple burdens. It was fairly related to services and protection offered stevedoring companies by the state and did not discriminate against interstate commerce. The principles embraced in *Complete Auto* thus exonerate the stevedoring tax of any commerce clause infirmity.

The import-export clause generally bars states from taxing imports or exports without congressional consent. The court explained in *Michelin Tire Corporation* v. *Wages,* 423 U.S. 276 (1976), that as applied to imports, the clause was intended to advance three policies: ensuring that the federal government could speak with a single voice in negotiating tariffs and foreign trade relations, offering the federal government a virtual monopoly over import revenues to support its operations, and fostering harmony among states that might be disturbed if seaboard states exacted heavy taxes on goods merely flowing through their ports of entry to the disadvantage of inland states. The tax on stevedoring offends none of these policies. It applies only to business conducted entirely within Washington and does not impede the regulation of foreign trade by the United States. Since the tax merely compensates the state for services and protection and is nondiscriminatory, its threat to federal import revenues through a reduction in demand for imported goods is minimal. The compensatory and nondiscriminatory characteristics of the tax will also forestall any significant interstate friction. Finally, the tax is not levied on imported goods but only on the business of loading and unloading ships. All

150

these considerations compel the conclusion that the tax is not a forbidden impost or duty within the meaning of the import-export
clause.

The constitutional prohibition against export taxes was intended
to vindicate the policies fostered by the ban against taxes on imports,
except for the protection of federal revenues. Federal taxes on exports
are constitutionally forbidden. The stevedoring tax, therefore, escapes reproach as an export tax for the reasons that absolve it of any
import tax infirmity.

United States Steel Corporation v. *Multistate Tax Commission*, 434 U.S. 452 (1978)

Facts: In *Northwestern States Portland Cement Co.* v. *Minnesota*, 358
U.S. 450 (1959), the Court held that net income from the interstate
operations of a foreign corporation may be subject to a state tax that
is both nondiscriminatory and fairly apportioned to local activities
that justify the exercise of the taxing power. In the wake of *Northwestern States*, several states drafted the Multistate Tax Compact to
simplify the administration of taxes levied against multistate businesses. It became effective in 1967 after its adoption by seven states,
but without congressional assent. The compact created the Multistate
Tax Commission, composed of tax administrators of member states,
which has a variety of powers: to recommend proposals for increasing
uniformity of tax laws, to publish information to assist states in implementing and taxpayers in complying with tax laws, to adopt advisory administrative regulations, and to perform an audit at the
request of a member state with the aid of compulsory process in
consenting states. Threatened with a tax audit by the commission,
U.S. Steel and several other multistate taxpayers brought suit, claiming that the compact was constitutionally infirm because it lacked the
consent of Congress as required by the compact clause, because it
burdened interstate commerce unreasonably, and because it violated
the rights of multistate taxpayers under the Fourteenth Amendment.
A three-judge federal district court rejected the arguments and denied
any relief.

Question: Does the Multistate Tax Compact violate either the
compact clause, Article I, Section 10, clause 3, or the commerce clause,
Article I, Section 8, clause 3 of the Constitution?

Decision: No. Opinion by Justice Powell. Vote: 7–2, White and
Blackmun dissenting.

151

Reasons: The compact clause provides that "No state shall, without the consent of Congress, . . . enter into any agreement or compact with another state, or with a foreign power." In earlier decisions the Court has disavowed a broad interpretation of the clause and has circumscribed its application to agreements that enhance state power at the expense of federal supremacy. The Multistate Tax Compact escapes the reach of the clause because it lacks any provisions that derogate from the powers of the United States. Member states retain complete freedom of sovereign action and may not exercise powers that would be unavailable without the compact. The compact neither increases state power to tax multistate or foreign business nor coerces nonmember states to alter their taxing procedures to conform to those of member states. Accordingly, the compact was outside the purview of the compact clause.

The commerce clause and Fourteenth Amendment attacks are equally ill conceived. They are founded on allegations that the commission induced member states to issue burdensome requests for documents from multistate businesses and to levy assessments in violation of state law. This alleged misconduct, however, can be ascribed only to individual states and is irrelevant to the facial validity of the compact.

Moorman Manufacturing Co. v. Bair, 437 U.S. 267 (1978)

Facts: As applied to interstate businesses, the Iowa corporate income tax is levied only on that portion of income "reasonably attributed" to business conducted within the state. If income is derived from the manufacture or sale of tangible personal property, it is presumed that the portion attributable to business in Iowa is the portion of total gross sales that were made in Iowa. If a taxpayer establishes that application of this single-factor sales formula would be inequitable, its taxable corporate income may be recalculated.

An Illinois corporation engaged in the manufacture and sale of animal feeds sold approximately 20 percent of its product in Iowa. It brought suit attacking the constitutionality of the single-factor sales formula on the grounds that it offended both constitutional due process and the commerce clause. The Supreme Court of Iowa rejected the attack.

Question: Does the single-factor sales formula employed by Iowa to apportion the income of an interstate business for income tax purposes violate either the due process clause or the commerce clause?

Decision: No. Opinion by Justice Stevens. Vote: 6–3, Brennan, Powell, and Blackmun dissenting.

Reasons: The due process clause offers a state broad discretion in attributing income to itself for purposes of taxing. In past decisions it has repeatedly been held that a single-factor formula similar to that employed by Iowa is presumptively valid. Due process precludes its application only when a taxpayer shows by clear and cogent evidence that it has yielded a grossly distorted result. Since the taxpayer in this case made no such showing, due process offered no protection against the single-factor sales formula.

The linchpin of the commerce clause attack is the alleged threat of duplicative taxation created by the Iowa formula. Because most states, including Illinois, use a three-factor formula based on property, payroll, and sales to apportion income, Iowa's single-factor formula enhances the risk that the income of an interstate business will be subject to multiple taxation. This risk, however, would not be eliminated even if Iowa embraced a three-factor formula. State rules for determining when a sale has occurred and for apportioning non-business income differ widely. To preclude any risk of duplicative taxation, national uniform rules for the division of all income must be embraced. Congress may enact such rules, but uniformity in state tax policies is not compelled by the commerce clause. It offers no justification for disturbing Iowa's single-factor formula, despite the variance of Iowa's formula from the three-factor formula used by most other states.

Baldwin v. Fish and Game Commission of Montana, 436 U.S. 371 (1978)

Facts: The Montana licensing scheme for regulating the recreational hunting of elk and other big game prefers residents over non-residents. The former may purchase elk-hunting licenses for $9, whereas the latter are required to purchase a $225 combination license to hunt not only elk but other game as well. A resident of Montana may obtain an equivalent combination license for $30. Nonresident hunters unsuccessfully attacked the licensing scheme in federal district court as constitutionally infirm under the privileges and immunities clause, Article IV, Section 2, clause 2, and the equal protection clause of the Fourteenth Amendment.

Question: Does the discrimination against nonresidents inflicted by the Montana big-game licensing scheme offend either the privileges and immunities clause or the equal protection clause?

153

Decision: No. Opinion by Justice Blackmun. Vote: 6–3, Brennan, White, and Marshall dissenting.

Reasons: The privileges and immunities clause establishes a norm of comity among states that demands equality of treatment of residents and nonresidents with respect to essential or fundamental rights. These include the right to pursue commercial activity or gainful employment, the right to own and dispose of private property, and the right to use state courts. The goal of the privileges and immunities clause is vindicated so long as states eschew discrimination against nonresidents in ways that "hinder the formation, the purpose, or the development of a single union of [individual] States" and that threaten "the vitality of the Nation as a single entity."

The contested discrimination against nonresidents in purchasing elk-hunting licenses in Montana does not threaten a basic right within the embrace of the privileges and immunities clause. Elk hunting by nonresidents is a costly sport, indulged in only by the wealthy. It does not involve commercial exploitation: "[t]he mastery of the animal and the trophy are the ends that are sought." Since nondiscrimination in the recreational hunting of Montana elk is not "basic to the maintenance or well-being of the Union," it is not a command of the privileges and immunities clause.

Montana's license-fee discrimination against nonresident hunters is also sufficiently rational to escape reproach under the equal protection clause. Residents, unlike nonresidents, pay taxes that assist in the acquisition and maintenance of the big-game population. The taxes support state parks, access roads, fire suppression, air- and water-quality programs, and highway patrol and wildlife officers to enforce game laws. The number of nonresident hunters, moreover, has recently increased more rapidly than the number of their resident counterparts, and the former generally pose greater problems of law enforcement. Finally, the contested license fees advance the state's legitimate interest in conserving its big-game population. These considerations bless the Montana license-fee structure with the rationality necessary to survive equal protection scrutiny.

> We perceive no duty on the State to have its licensing structure parallel or identical for both residents and nonresidents, or to justify to the penny any cost differential it imposes in a purely recreational, noncommercial, nonlivelihood setting.

INDEX OF CASES

SUBJECT INDEX